RESEARCHING
DAILY LIFE

RESEARCHING
DAILY LIFE

a guide to EXPERIENCE SAMPLING
and DAILY DIARY METHODS

PAUL J. SILVIA
KATHERINE N. COTTER

 AMERICAN PSYCHOLOGICAL ASSOCIATION

Copyright © 2021 by the American Psychological Association. All rights reserved. Except as permitted under the United States Copyright Act of 1976, no part of this publication may be reproduced or distributed in any form or by any means, including, but not limited to, the process of scanning and digitization, or stored in a database or retrieval system, without the prior written permission of the publisher.

The opinions and statements published are the responsibility of the authors, and such opinions and statements do not necessarily represent the policies of the American Psychological Association.

Published by
American Psychological Association
750 First Street, NE
Washington, DC 20002
https://www.apa.org

Order Department
https://www.apa.org/pubs/books
order@apa.org

In the U.K., Europe, Africa, and the Middle East, copies may be ordered from Eurospan
https://www.eurospanbookstore.com/apa
info@eurospangroup.com

Typeset in Charter and Interstate by Circle Graphics, Inc., Reisterstown, MD

Printer: Sheridan Books, Chelsea, MI
Cover Designer: Mark Karis

Library of Congress Cataloging-in-Publication Data

Names: Silvia, Paul J., 1976- author. | Cotter, Katherine N., author.
Title: Researching daily life : a guide to experience sampling and daily
  diary methods / by Paul J. Silvia and Katherine N. Cotter.
Description: Washington, DC : American Psychological Association, [2021] |
  Includes bibliographical references and index.
Identifiers: LCCN 2020039243 (print) | LCCN 2020039244 (ebook) |
  ISBN 9781433834578 (paperback) | ISBN 9781433835629 (ebook)
Subjects: LCSH: Experiential research—Methodology. | Human behavior—
  Research—Methodology. | Psychology—Research—Methodology. |
  Social sciences—Research—Methodology.
Classification: LCC BF76.6.E94 S55 2021 (print) | LCC BF76.6.E94 (ebook) |
  DDC 150.72/3—dc23
LC record available at https://lccn.loc.gov/2020039243
LC ebook record available at https://lccn.loc.gov/2020039244

https://doi.org/10.1037/0000236-000

Printed in the United States of America

10 9 8 7 6 5 4 3 2 1

Contents

Preface *vii*
Acknowledgments *xi*

1. What Are Daily Life Methods?   3
Three Defining Features of Daily Life Methods   *4*
Comparing Daily Life Methods With Other Popular Methods   *12*
Apt Research Questions for Daily Life Methods   *14*
Conclusion   *15*

2. Choosing a Sampling Design   17
Sampling From Daily Life   *17*
Event-Based Sampling   *19*
Fixed-Interval Sampling   *22*
Random-Interval Sampling   *27*
All of the Above: Combining Sampling Designs   *31*
Conclusion   *33*

3. Designing Self-Report Surveys   35
The Trade-Offs Among Items, Beeps, and Days   *36*
Developing Items   *38*
Survey Features   *46*
Measurement Reactivity   *48*
Conclusion   *51*

4. Selecting a System for Signals and Surveys — 53
   1. Does the System Send Signals, Collect Data, or Both? — 54
   2. Is the Equipment Yours or Theirs? — 55
   3. Can Participants Ignore or Control the Signal? — 58
   4. How Does Time Get Stamped? — 59
   5. Do Missed Surveys Vanish? — 61
   6. How Convenient Is the Survey Process for Participants? — 62
   7. What Are the Initial and Ongoing Costs? — 63
   8. Does It Suit the Participants and Their Environments? — 64
   9. How Much Training Will Personnel and Participants Need? — 65
   10. How Private Is Data Collection, and How Secure Are the Data? — 65
   Conclusion — 67

5. Collecting Data — 69
   Preparing to Run the Study — 70
   Running the Study — 83
   Improving Response Rates and Data Quality — 89
   Conclusion — 92

6. Cleaning and Processing Your Data — 93
   Organizing Your Data — 93
   Assessing Data Quality — 102
   Conclusion — 109

7. Analyzing Daily Life Data — 111
   Some Peculiar Qualities of Daily Life Data — 112
   Some Vexing Issues — 119
   Conclusion — 125

8. Presenting and Publishing Your Research — 127
   Presenting Daily Life Research — 128
   Publishing Daily Life Research — 131
   Conclusion — 138

References — 139
Index — 157
About the Authors — 165

Preface

All research methods are harder than they look—even the simplest methods have small details to master and big potholes to avoid. Nevertheless, some kinds of research have higher barriers to entry than others: Aspiring researchers need more skills, training, and knowledge to get started. Methods with low barriers to entry, such as online surveys and simple experiments with convenience samples of adults, are what we teach to undergraduates and see at student-only poster sessions at regional conferences. Methods with high barriers to entry, such as functional neuroimaging, clinical trials, meta-analyses, and computational modeling, take years of graduate and postdoctoral training to learn.

Daily life methods, the topic of this book, fall somewhere in between. In our years of conducting, presenting, and teaching daily diary and experience sampling methods, we've found that newcomers are often unnecessarily intimidated or dangerously overconfident. Some researchers see these methods as more intricate and delicate than they are, so they're reluctant to take the leap. Although a daily diary study is more complex than a one-shot online survey, it isn't rocket surgery. The more serious problem, we've found, is overconfidence. Researchers see a cool experience-sampling talk at a conference, get excited to try it, and think, "How hard can it be? I already know how to give surveys—it's just giving more of them." The rise of sophisticated smartphone applications and online platforms has fueled an impulsive "there's an app for that" mindset that ends in vexation and calamity.

Our aim in this book is to teach you how to do daily life research: how to think about the method, design a study, develop suitable assessments, collect data, and disseminate your findings. We assume a background in the basics of research methods but not much more. We intend the book to be suitable for advanced undergraduates working as research assistants, graduate students getting started with their own projects, postdocs entering a daily-life lab, and established researchers wanting to add some tools to the toolbox.

Our goal in this book is to walk researchers through the process of designing and conducting a daily life project. Our focus is on the classic, prototypical kinds of projects—studies that sample at least once a day and collect self-report data. On the design side, we emphasize daily diaries and within-day experience sampling. These are the most common designs and the building blocks of more intricate projects. On the measurement side, we emphasize self-report items—daily life surveys—that participants complete in their daily environments. Self-report surveys are both the most common kind of daily life assessment and the best place for new researchers to start.

If this book has a cornerstone message, it is that your first project should be straightforward and focused on the fundamentals. The world of daily life methods is innovative and ever expanding, and we realize that it's tempting to jump into a complicated study using the latest wearable devices and ambulatory sensors. But just as we walk before we run, we conduct a basic self-report study before we wire participants with limb accelerometers, mobile eye trackers, and impedance cardiographs that send electricity through thoracic electrodes. Once mastered, the fundamentals are easily extended to advanced designs and high-tech assessment tools. Do a simple first study, work out the kinks, and scale up from there.

As with all research methods, daily life methods have fundamental principles of design, sampling, and assessment that must be understood before diving into data collection. Throughout the book, we discuss many topics that might seem glaringly obvious or needlessly subtle, but our goal is to reveal the many "unknown unknowns" of daily life research. Our hope is that by this book's end, readers will think at least once, "Now that's a pothole I would've stepped in."

In the following chapters, we'll walk through the life cycle of a daily life project, from conception to publication. Chapter 1 introduces the animating features of daily life research: real-time, repeated assessment of people in their natural environments. Chapter 2 describes how to create a *sampling design*: your plan for when and how often to assess people. Daily life work has developed a handful of core sampling designs that suit different kinds of research questions. Once you have your design, you need to develop assessments. Items that work in one-shot surveys rarely work as-is when used dozens of times to describe momentary events and experiences. Chapter 3 describes how to write good items for intensive, real-world use.

To launch your project, you need a system for signaling participants and collecting data. Chapter 4 describes how to select a system by describing 10 questions to ask about your project, participants, and resources. Chapter 5 turns to the nuts and bolts of collecting data, with a focus on good methodological practices that yield higher response rates and cleaner data. Once data collection ends, you will experience the feral beauty of raw daily life data. Chapter 6 provides advice for cleaning and processing the data to prepare it for analysis, and Chapter 7 describes quirky analytic issues to be aware of when planning your statistical analyses. Many readers already have the tools and skills to model daily life data, but we think many others should consider bringing in a statistical collaborator. Finally, when the dust settles, it will be time to share your findings with the world. Chapter 8 concludes our book by discussing good practices for presenting daily life projects as posters and talks and for developing manuscripts to submit to peer-reviewed journals.

Acknowledgments

Many hands make light the work, even when only four of them are doing the typing. We appreciate the crew at American Psychological Association (APA) Books for bringing this book into the world. Linda Malnasi McCarter deserves extra thanks for helping us shape and sharpen the book's concept and for well-timed texts and memes. Our background in daily life methods would not have been possible without funding from several federal agencies (the National Institutes of Health, Department of Education, and Department of Veterans Affairs) and private organizations (The Imagination Institute and Psi Chi); we're grateful for their support of our work. Finally, daily life work requires a team, and we owe an enormous debt of thanks to our many collaborators on our daily life projects over the years; Tom Kwapil, partner in our earliest experience sampling crimes, deserves special thanks and probably a few apologies. None of them is responsible for whatever wayward or wacky ideas that might have wandered into this book.

RESEARCHING
DAILY LIFE

1 WHAT ARE DAILY LIFE METHODS?

What are you doing right now? You needn't be a mind-reading psychologist to make a good guess—you're reading our book, presumably—but where are you? Who, if anyone, is around? What are you thinking about? What's your mood like? What has happened so far today? And what do you expect to do later? (Finish reading our book, we hope.)

A large community of researchers has a passionate and nosy interest in what people are doing in their ordinary environments in their everyday lives. Some researchers are interested in mundane, ordinary events—the ones that make up most of our lives—for their own sake. Others study real-world experiences because that's where you find clinical symptoms and problem behaviors—where people experience pain, crave nicotine, drink to excess, sleep poorly, think about hurting themselves, and argue with their partners. The real world is also where you'll find the brighter side of behavior—where people feel hopeful, use their imagination, achieve their goals, enjoy the great outdoors, create new things, and connect with people they care about.

Once a niche side of psychology, the study of daily life has developed into a major research tradition and transformed translational fields like clinical psychology, health psychology, and behavioral medicine (Conner et al., 2009; Robbins & Kubiak, 2014; Trull & Ebner-Priemer, 2013; Wheeler & Reis, 1991). In this chapter, we describe the fundamentals of daily life methods: their defining features, core assumptions, and typical applications. We conclude by contrasting them with familiar methods, like experimental, survey, and longitudinal methods, to sharpen your understanding of the unique advantages and drawbacks of daily life research.

THREE DEFINING FEATURES OF DAILY LIFE METHODS

Daily life methods go by many names. Some are well known, like *experience sampling* and *ecological momentary assessment*. Others are niche or quirky, like *beeper studies* and *real-time data capture*. Exhibit 1.1 describes the most common labels for this family of research methods; most of them will sound familiar. Just as language speakers coin new words to capture different shades of complex concepts, researchers coin new labels for diverse fields of scholarship. Each label in Exhibit 1.1 captures a different facet of the method and reflects the emphasis of a subgroup of researchers. Some labels emphasize that sampling happens in the real world; others emphasize the longitudinal quality of repeated assessment; still others emphasize real-time measurement. A few labels reflect historical events, like the popularity of pagers and Palm Pilots in pioneering research.

No one label neatly covers the many research traditions that use these methods. In this book, we adopt Mehl and Conner's (2012) choice of the term *daily life methods* to capture this sprawling family. We think the term is apt for positioning daily life methods within psychology's broader panoply of research tools. For most newcomers, the most intriguing—and often the most intimidating—feature of this research is that it happens in people's natural habitats. Learning to do daily life research requires moving away from the comfort zone of the lab—with all the control, precision, and standardization it affords—and into the participants' diverse, complex, and occasionally raucous daily environments. To researchers new to these methods, learning to collect data from participants in their own environments is the most salient feature of the method and the biggest barrier to getting started.

Whatever you call it, this family of methods has three defining features (Stone et al., 2007):

1. People are assessed in their *natural environments*. Daily life research favors assessing people in the messy real world, not the tidy research lab or clinic.

EXHIBIT 1.1. Some Common Labels for Daily Life Methods

- **Ecological momentary assessment.** Known as *EMA*, this term is probably the most common global label. Particularly prominent in clinical, medical, and health research, EMA emphasizes the goals of collecting data that are both real world (ecological) and real time (momentary) in nature.

- **Experience sampling methods.** Usually called simply *ESM*, this label comes from the research tradition that emphasizes frequent random sampling of momentary subjective experiences, such as describing one's moods and activities every few hours for a week. It is rooted in the pioneering work of Mihaly Csikszentmihalyi (1975) and his collaborators.

- **Diary research.** This label is most common in studies that collect surveys once a day, known as *daily diary studies*, and those that administer and collect surveys each time a focal event happens (see Chapter 2 for more details).

- **Ambulatory assessment.** This label appears in the name of the field's major scholarly society—the Society for Ambulatory Assessment (https://www.ambulatory-assessment.org). A particularly prominent term in European research, ambulatory assessment emphasizes data collection that occurs as people move naturally through their daily environments. This term is especially apt for projects that use portable devices to assess biological outcomes, such as ambulatory assessment of blood pressure and heart rate variability (Houtveen & de Geus, 2009).

- **Intensive longitudinal methods.** This label emphasizes the distinctive methodological quality of daily life research. People are assessed over time, as in all longitudinal studies, but the assessments are dense (e.g., once a day for 30 days) instead of sparse (e.g., twice a year for 4 years).

- **Real-time data capture.** This label is most common in the tradition of research on passive, continuous sensing, such as studies that measure environmental features (e.g., ambient noise and temperature), physiological variables (e.g., heart rate), and behavioral factors (e.g., movement, eye tracking, and GPS location).

- **Beeper research.** Early experience sampling work used pagers (i.e., beepers) and digital watches that would make a retro, 1980s-style beeping sound to signal people to complete a survey. Although the term is now archaic, modern researchers still use *beep* as a shorthand for *signal* or *occasion* (e.g., "Participants were beeped four times a day to complete a survey").

- **Palm Pilot research.** Older readers might remember Palm Pilots, which were like black-and-white smartphones that couldn't make calls, send texts, take pictures, or connect to the internet. When loaded with special-purpose software (Le et al., 2006), however, Palm Pilots could both signal participants and administer surveys. Their ability to both send signals and collect data made them wildly popular, so this now-outdated label stuck as a shorthand for the family of experience sampling methods.

2. Researchers aspire to *real-time assessment*—measuring events and experiences close to when they happen.
3. Instead of giving a survey once, researchers *intensively assess* people over time—often one to 10 times daily for many consecutive days. Each participant provides a large sample of thoughts, actions, and emotions in a small time frame.

Natural Environments

Why do daily life researchers study people in their natural environments? Why is it worth the hassle? We can see the virtues and flaws of studying people in the real world by flipping the question: Why do we study people in the lab? Why do we ask participants to come to our research labs and clinics to provide data? One ignoble virtue of lab research is that it's convenient. We researchers work in our labs, so it's easier for us to ask participants to come to where the staff, equipment, and grimy coffee mugs are. Convenience aside, our scientific tools may be too fragile, bulky, or risky to take into the field. Few magnetic resonance imaging scanners have wheels.

The primary virtue of lab research, however, is control. Research labs are rarely glamorous places, but they afford a predictable, stable, and standardized environment for collecting data. Environmental distractions—noise, visual distractions, passersby—can be minimized, and the environment is held constant across experimental conditions and participants. Studying small effects requires sanding down as many sources of error as possible, and nothing beats the controlled environment of a lab for that.

For the lab environment to accomplish what it does, it needs to differ from the usual environments that people spend time in. Labs are quiet, innocuous, and constrained, with social norms that nudge participants to put away their phones, pay attention to instructions, and take the procedure relatively seriously. From their perspective, participants experience the lab environment as formal and odd: They're under a microscope, working on unfamiliar tasks, and unable to do much else for a certain amount of time. By design, a lab environment affords few behavioral degrees of freedom for participants. As Reis (2012) pointed out, "in a laboratory cubicle, participants can do little else but complete the tasks assigned to them by researchers as quickly as possible" (p. 13).

In short, the typical lab isn't a neutral environment. The physical environment surely varies—some researchers have nice space, and others toil in a hovel of cinder blocks and flickering fluorescent tubes—but it's the social–behavioral environment that makes research labs unique for participants. To a daily life researcher, the research lab is merely one of many environments their participants entered that day. Once they leave, never to return, the participants fan out into a quirky range of environments: a bedroom they decorated themselves, their medieval history class, an outdoor park, the local museum, their car, or another stressful shift at the restaurant.

All research methods have trade-offs. In lab research, we trade realism for control. It's the right trade-off to make when we need controlled conditions but don't need realism. Daily life researchers take the other side of the trade: We trade control for realism so we can illuminate the richness and diversity of people's everyday worlds. Daily-life methods are animated by curiosity about what people's ecosystems are like. When people can do whatever they want, what do they do? How do they spend their time? What are their inner lives and social worlds like?

We've found that researchers new to daily life methods will fret when the findings from their first daily life study diverge from what they found in the lab. But don't worry—it would be weird to find the same thing, and you should expect the findings to vary. As one example, consider research on Openness to Experience, a broad factor of personality associated with imagination, fantasy, and vivid inner experience (Christensen, 2020). When cognitive psychology examines mind-wandering in the lab, such as how often people have task-unrelated thoughts during computerized cognitive tasks, Openness to Experience is essentially unrelated to how often people mind-wander (Kane et al., 2017). But when mind-wandering is studied in the real world using experience sampling, people high in Openness to Experience mind-wander much more often (Kane et al., 2017).

Neither finding is "wrong"—each reflects how people high in Openness to Experience behave in different environments. When sitting in a quiet, unfamiliar lab room with nothing to do but focus on a cognitive task and respond with a keyboard, they turn their efforts to the task. But when they're immersed in their quirky everyday lives, free to focus on more meaningful goals and experiences, their vivid imaginations will roam (Oleynick et al., 2017). An animating assumption in daily life research is that the research lab is but one of many contexts—it isn't the default, baseline, ideal, or benchmark against which all other methods are compared. The point of doing work outside the lab is the suspicion, if not the hope, that the findings will vary—in their direction, structure, or complexity—when you leave your lab and study people where they are.

Real-Time Data Collection

Daily life research emphasizes *real-time data collection*—measuring events as they happen (Schwartz, 2012). In practice, real-time responding is an aspiration, something that research projects approximate but rarely attain. In some studies, researchers can measure variables in literal real time. Many physiological and environmental factors—heart rate, air temperature, and ambient noise, for example—can be sampled many times per second without the participant's input (see Exhibit 1.2). For studies using self-report assessment, however, it's more accurate to say that daily life methods use *near-term data collection*: They measure people's experiences close to when they happen. The gap from event to response ranges from under a minute in experience sampling studies, which interrupt ongoing activity for immediate reports, to most of a waking day in daily diary studies, which collect end-of-day responses that describe the day's events (see Chapter 2, this volume).

Retrospective self-reports are the salient contrast for real-time assessment. The typical, off-the-shelf questionnaire asks people to think about themselves and their past to generate a number that describes it. The number might represent frequency information (e.g., how often, in a typical month, people exercise, drink alcohol, eat a serving of fish, or have a bad day at work) or for qualities of experience (e.g., ratings on a Likert scale for the typical intensity

---

EXHIBIT 1.2. Outcomes Beyond Self-Reports

Self-reports are by far the most common source of data in daily life research, but this fast-moving field adds new tools every year. We list here some examples of outcomes beyond self-reports that you might consider learning.

Environmental Variables
- Air temperature
- Lighting
- Ambient sound and noise exposure
- GPS location

Biobehavioral Variables
- Autonomic outcomes: heart rate, blood pressure, respiration, heart rate variability, cardiac systolic intervals, skin conductance
- Endocrine outcomes: glucose, cortisol, alpha-amylase, oxytocin
- Eye tracking
- Posture
- Frequency and rate of speech
- Movement and activity level
- Sleep periods

of joint pain, their global life satisfaction, their average sleep quality, or their overall emotional closeness with their partner). People will always give you a number when asked, but one wonders how people arrive at numbers for events and behaviors that they haven't tracked, rarely pay attention to, and often try to avoid thinking about. People are busy, frazzled, and distracted by their phones, so we can forgive them if they haven't been keeping track of the number of positive interactions they had with their spouse last week, how many servings of nuts they ate, and how many hours they spent distracted by their phone.

How people answer questions about their past behaviors and experiences is a fascinating topic of research in its own right (Stone et al., 1999; Tourangeau et al., 2000). A clear theme in the science of self-reports is that researchers shouldn't expect much when they ask people to pool their complex and varied experiences over time and distill them into a number. People can be much more accurate for some kinds of questions and experiences than others, but people's retrospective judgments are strongly influenced by events that are especially recent, salient, or intense; by mental models of the world and personal theories of what they are like; and by a range of self-serving and self-enhancing tendencies (Schwartz, 2012; Tourangeau et al., 2000).

Retrospective self-reports have their virtues, but if you want to know what daily experience is like—how often something happened, what the situation was like when it occurred, and how people experienced it—you need to assess things close to when they happen. Daily life research uses a few core sampling designs, explained in Chapter 2, that represent different strategies for catching what's happening in people's lives. Some studies interrupt people as they go about their day and ask about the present moment; other studies collect self-reports at fixed intervals, such as every 4 hours or every evening; and still other studies collect reports whenever a focal event happens. Their differences aside, these sampling designs all seek to reduce biases associated with remembering and tracking one's experiences.

Minimizing recall biases isn't the only strength of real-time assessment. Many things we want to study are so fleeting or subtle that people may not notice an experience, reflect on it, or label it. When asked later for global self-reports, they somehow must describe experiences that went unnoticed. The issue of *metaconsciousness*—the conscious awareness of conscious states (Schooler, 2002)—is a major motivation for real-time assessment. For example, people can have intense thoughts and experiences (e.g., urges connected to self-harm or disordered eating) without additionally thinking about and labeling those experiences ("That's the kind of thought I talked about with my therapist yesterday"). People usually go about their day in a cheery mood without reflectively thinking, "I feel pretty cheery right now." Much mental imagery, from elaborate daydreams to hearing music in one's head, is consciously experienced but not metaconsciously experienced ("Why am I hearing 'Don't Stop Believin' again?"). The best way to assess fleeting, fast-moving experiences is to catch them as they happen.

Intensive Assessment Over Time

Repeated assessments are the third defining quality of daily life research. Many research methods use repeated assessments—longitudinal studies of development being a classic example—but daily life methods crank the knob to 11. Instead of assessing people once or twice a year, daily life projects assess people at least once a day and often at least once an hour. This kind of repeated assessment is often labeled "dense" or "intensive" (Bolger & Laurenceau, 2013): It seeks a big sample from a small period of time.

Some benefits of intensive, repeated sampling are obvious. If you want to study change, for example, the repeated sampling inherent in longitudinal designs will allow you to examine patterns of growth and change. Because it is interested in change over tiny time scales—a week, a day, an hour—daily life research must intensively sample to ensure it catches the fast-moving targets it studies. Many clinical and health constructs, for example, change during the day, often rapidly. It's common for experiences of pain, stiffness, energy, alertness, and affect to vary across the waking day (Bellamy et al., 2004; Palmer, 2002; Watson, 2000). Many activities during the day—eating, exercising, arguing, stressing—spark interesting near-term consequences (e.g., isolating oneself, having cravings, or experiencing thoughts of self-harm) that are captured only with dense assessments.

Not all daily life studies are interested in temporal trends, though. Many use dense, repeated assessment to build up a large sample of each individual person's thoughts, actions, and experiences. Just as a 10-item scale will yield more reliable scores than a three-item scale, all else equal, sampling 60 times from someone's week will yield more precise estimates than six times—and both are probably better than asking for a global, retrospective judgment. Intensive assessment builds up big within-person sample sizes, which then allow researchers to make good estimates of the *frequency* and *quality* of daily experience. For frequency information, repeated assessment yields good estimates for how often something happened during the study.

If you want to know how often people smoked cigarettes, studied for a class, had stressful interactions at work, drank excessively, or practiced a skill they learned in treatment, intensive assessments will yield good frequency estimates. For qualitative information, repeated assessments illuminate people's average levels of the construct of interest, whether it's how well they slept last night to how strongly they crave nicotine.

Once you have a large distribution of experiences for a particular person, you can do more than just estimate the central tendency. The next step is to explore within-person variability: how much people vary around their own means, and why. Daily life researchers find the variability of a given person's experiences fascinating. We know that many psychological constructs vary widely within a single person's typical day. Daily life studies of moods and emotions, for example, show that a person's emotional states can vary greatly during a day (Eaton & Funder, 2001), that people show diurnal cycles in affect (Watson, 2000), and that many mood disorders are marked by volatile emotional experiences (Ebner-Priemer et al., 2009). For other psychological constructs, we might suspect interesting within-person variability but can find it only with intensive sampling. For example, people show many interesting circaseptal (7-day) trends in their emotions, activities, and goals that are apparent in daily diary studies that stretch across many weeks (Larsen & Kasimatis, 1990), and for some psychological constructs, few people expect to see meaningful within-person variability until daily life projects reveal it (e.g., expressions of personality traits; Fleeson, 2004).

Once you have enough observations to estimate means and variances of a person's experiences, the natural next step is to explain within-person variability in the experiences. Why does positive affect vary so much within a day? What other predictors that also vary within a day might explain within-person variance in positive affect? We know, to name a few examples, that fluctuations in daily mood are associated with biobehavioral variables (e.g., time since awakening, what people recently ate or drank), social factors (e.g., being alone vs. spending time with other people), and motivational processes (e.g., making progress on meaningful goals) that themselves vary throughout a day. Many daily life projects go a step further by exploring the time structure of within-person relationships, such as whether the effects of one experience (e.g., positive and negative emotions early in the day) show up at later time points (e.g., heavy drinking later that night; Wray et al., 2014). In short, you can learn a lot about a person if you have a large sample of the person's experiences to work with.

COMPARING DAILY LIFE METHODS WITH OTHER POPULAR METHODS

How do daily life methods compare with other popular methods in the social and behavioral sciences? Here's how daily life research is like and unlike experimental methods, survey methods, and longitudinal methods.

Experimental Methods

Experimental methods manipulate variables and observe their effects. Although experiments are not necessarily conducted in the lab, research labs are the natural habitat for experimental designs because they usually must hold many factors constant that are hard to wrangle in the field. Daily life studies happen outside the lab, but they can apply experimental methods. Many daily life studies manipulate between-person factors and randomly assign participants to conditions. Methodological studies, for example, have manipulated the length of surveys (Eisele et al., 2020) or the kinds of devices participants used (Burgin et al., 2012).

Experiments that test in situ interventions—known as *ecological momentary interventions*—are fascinating examples of the integration of experimental and ecological methods (Carter et al., 2007; McDevitt-Murphy et al., 2018). The typical daily life project, however, is correlational, focusing on the natural covariation of factors of interest. If anything, daily life projects tend to be doubly correlational: They are interested in between-person correlations (how features of people covary in a sample of people) and within-person correlations (how features of experiences covary in a sample of occasions).

Survey Methods

The prototypical survey project is cross-sectional: It seeks to understand a large group of people at a single point in time. For quality surveys, such as projects designed to guide high-stakes decisions, the sampling design and recruiting methods are carefully crafted to enable valid claims about a broader population of people (Henry, 1990). Most survey studies in the social and behavioral sciences, however, are cross-sectional studies of haphazardly recruited groups, usually quota samples and convenience samples (Silvia, 2020). Survey research with such samples is affordable and easy, so it isn't a bad place to start when exploring a new idea.

You can think of daily life methods as a quirky kind of survey project. The typical daily life study does give participants self-report surveys about what they are doing and thinking. The key difference is the design. Survey projects seek to understand a large group of *people* by studying them once, usually by asking for global, retrospective self-reports. Daily life projects, in contrast, seek to understand a large group of *occasions*: events and experiences that occurred during the project period. Daily life designs are akin to multistage sampling: Researchers first obtain a sample of people and then obtain a sample of those people's emotions, thoughts, and actions using intensive, repeated surveys about real-time events.

Longitudinal Methods

Longitudinal methods are the cornerstone of fields interested in change, growth, and development. The stereotypical longitudinal study follows a group of people over a long period of time, usually years, but any study with repeated, time-structured assessments is longitudinal. Daily life studies, by sampling people repeatedly, certainly qualify. You can view daily life projects as studies that seek a fine-grained view of a small span of time: how adults consume alcohol on weekend nights (Kuntsche & Cooper, 2010), how polydrug users experience cravings and use illicit substances (Hopper et al., 2006), or how adults with depression engage with therapy-related goals in between sessions (Hoet et al., 2018). A stereotypical longitudinal project, in contrast, seeks a broader view of a large span of time, usually with assessments spaced by months or years. The label *intensive longitudinal methods* (see Exhibit 1.1) calls attention to the high density of daily life assessment.

Another way that daily life studies differ from typical longitudinal studies is the cardinal role of time. Longitudinal research is animated by understanding how psychological systems grow, evolve, and change. It sounds obvious, but time is the star of the show, the fundamental predictor, in longitudinal projects. In daily life projects, however, time per se may be unimportant. The data are collected intensively over time, often yielding many dozens of repeated measurements, but time might be peripheral to the research questions. Many daily life projects are interested in how processes unfold over small time scales, but in many others time is incidental. When the focus of a project is on understanding how often something happens or how within-person variables covary, the temporal order of the data is usually viewed as a nuisance to control for or ignore (see Chapter 6). All daily life projects thus have longitudinal assessments, but they do not necessarily have longitudinal hypotheses about growth and change across time.

APT RESEARCH QUESTIONS FOR DAILY LIFE METHODS

All research methods have trade-offs and sweet spots; there's no single best method for all research questions. Now that we've learned the fundamental features of daily life methods and drawn contrasts with other methods, what are apt research questions for daily life research? For what kinds of problems are daily life methods suitable? Here are some of the most common kinds of questions in published daily life research:

- *How often does something happen?* Research questions focused on the prevalence of activities and experiences in people's daily lives are a great match. If you want to know how often something happens, real-time tracking over a preset interval will be much more revealing than simply asking people, "In a typical week, how often do you . . .?"

- *How variable is an experience?* The "amount" of an outcome reveals little about its variability. Daily life methods, because of their intensive, repeated assessments, are well suited to reveal variability, dispersion, and diversity in a person's experiences and activities.

- *Does a variable have a temporal trend or pattern?* Repeated assessments over time can shed light on a variable's time structure. Questions about short-term temporal trends and patterns are perfect for daily life methods. We've mentioned several examples already, such as circadian and circaseptal trends in emotion (Larsen & Kasimatis, 1990; Watson, 2000).

- *Are two variables related within person?* How do variables relate at the within-person level (Hamaker, 2012)? As a person's mood changes, for example, what else changes with it? Intensive, repeated assessment lets one look at within-person relationships, including concurrent and time-lagged relationships.

- *Do people differ in how often something happens?* After collecting a large pool of responses, you can examine how between-person factors—such as group memberships, clinical status, and personality traits—predict the frequency of the event.

- *Do people differ in the level or amount of an experience?* A similar question concerns between-person main effects on levels of variables, such as whether personality traits predict the levels of outcomes like positive affect, loneliness, and activity levels.

- *Do people differ in their variability?* A less common research question—but one perfect for daily life methods—is whether between-person variables predict differences in variability. Often the interesting action is in the variability, not the mean levels. With a large pool of responses, you can examine predictors of dispersion and variance, such as whether some clinical features predict exaggerated or dampened variability in emotion, sleep, or social activity.

- *Do within-person effects, like trends or relationships, vary between people?* Most projects involve a mix of within-person and between-person research questions, so exploring questions about their interactions is natural. Such effects, known as *cross-level interactions*, examine whether a within-person effect varies across people. For example, the within-person effect of social interaction on positive mood might be stronger for some people and weaker for others; likewise, a temporal trend, such as the effect of time of day on positive affect, alertness, or cortisol level, may be stronger or weaker for some people or groups.

This list isn't exhaustive, but these classic, prototypical questions should spark some ideas for how you can apply daily life methods to your research domain.

CONCLUSION

Once a niche set of tools, daily life methods have evolved into a popular family of methods used throughout the psychological, clinical, and health sciences. In this chapter we have reviewed the defining features of daily life research—real-time, repeated assessment of people in their natural environments—and considered some research questions that lend themselves to daily life methods. If you're ready to take the plunge into daily life research, in Chapter 2 we explain the first step in designing a project: choosing a sampling design.

2 CHOOSING A SAMPLING DESIGN

When we think about *sampling* in research, we usually think about sampling people from a population of interest. In daily life research, we have two layers of sampling. We do sample people, of course, by recruiting them to take part in our research project, but we then go on to sample from their daily lives. This deeper layer of sampling—how to capture what the participants were doing, thinking, and feeling in their normal environments—is the focus of this chapter. We describe the most common sampling designs in daily life research, appraise their strengths and weaknesses, and explain the kinds of questions for which they are best suited.

SAMPLING FROM DAILY LIFE

In psychological research, sampling is motivated by our research goals and constrained by practical realities. The reason why we "sample" people in the first place is because we can't measure the whole population, which is usually too big, dispersed, or inaccessible for us to assess exhaustively

---

https://doi.org/10.1037/0000236-002
Researching Daily Life: A Guide to Experience Sampling and Daily Diary Methods, by P. J. Silvia and K. N. Cotter
Copyright © 2021 by the American Psychological Association. All rights reserved.

(Silvia, 2020). Instead, researchers seek to assess a group of people—a subset of the population—in a way that is nevertheless informative, useful, and practical.

In daily life studies, the population is not a group of people but something more complex and ineluctable: a group of events, experiences, thoughts, and feelings across a lived, waking day. Researchers obviously can't assess the totality of someone's day even if they wanted to, so we need a sampling strategy—a way of assessing bits and pieces of the day—motivated by our research goals.

In some studies, we want to go deep into a narrow slice of daily life. Just as survey research sometimes wants to sample a narrow slice of a group of people—only people newly released from prison, only parents of bilingual children, or only psychology majors—sometimes daily life researchers are interested in a small slice of daily life. Instead of wanting to learn about the entire waking day, we want to isolate *focal events*, such as those snippets of the day when people disciplined a child, exercised, drank alcohol, or did something creative. A study focused on cigarette smoking, for example, might seek to collect data after each and every time people smoked during the day, thus allowing the researcher to ask questions about what people were doing, thinking, and feeling before, during, and after smoking. It's a good way to understand the experience of smoking and what it looks like in the real world.

In other studies, we want to go broad by casting a big net over daily life. Just as survey research sometimes seeks representative samples of a large and diverse population, sometimes daily life researchers want a representative snapshot of people's diverse and quirky days. These studies collect data repeatedly, often across many days and weeks, to develop a well-rounded sense of what people are doing, thinking, and feeling during their days.

In short, narrow and broad sampling fit different kinds of research goals. Narrow sampling targets specific slices of the day, usually discrete events. This approach yields fine detail about a small set of people's experiences and much less detail about the rest of the day. Broad sampling, in contrast, provides less detailed information about a much wider range of the day. Narrow and broad sampling simply represent two kinds of trade-offs that researchers can make. You can learn a lot about a little (narrow sampling) or a little about a lot (broad sampling). Both represent sweet spots for data collection depending on your research question.

These two levels of detail imply two main strategies for sampling from someone's day: (a) sampling based on *what*, known as *event-based sampling*; and (b) sampling based on *when*, known as *time-based sampling* (Shiffman, 2007). Event-based sampling collects data based on what happens: People are asked to provide data if a focal event occurred, such as after smoking a cigarette, exercising, arguing with a spouse, engaging in disordered eating behaviors, or rehearsing a musical performance. People fill out surveys only when the focal event happens, so this approach is used when researchers want to isolate and examine a narrow piece of people's daily experience.

Time-based sampling, on the other hand, collects data based on the passage of time: People provide data according to a fixed schedule (e.g., every hour, every 4 hours, or once per day before bedtime) or a random schedule (e.g., 10 surveys at random times between 8:00 a.m. and 10:00 p.m.). People fill out surveys regardless of whether anything of note took place, so this approach is used to capture the breadth and complexity of what people do, think, and feel throughout their days.

Most modern work uses one of three sampling designs: *event-based sampling*, *fixed-interval sampling*, and *random-interval sampling*. Although they occasionally go by different labels, these three designs are the basic building blocks of daily life research. After describing and unpacking them, we describe how these basic designs can be combined into more complex designs that harness their unique strengths.

EVENT-BASED SAMPLING

Event-based sampling asks people to provide data when a focal event happens. By asking people for details about the event—what it was like, where and when it happened, and what preceded it—researchers can learn how often something happens in someone's daily life and capture what the experience was like. This approach is ubiquitous in health research because health-relevant behaviors are often discrete events—people either consumed alcohol or they didn't—and because people's retrospective reports of healthy and unhealthy behaviors aren't entirely trustworthy (see Chapter 1). Here are a couple examples of what event-based sampling looks like in practice:

- For 4 weeks, a sample of women who meet subthreshold criteria for anorexia or bulimia nervosa completed a brief survey after each instance of eating-disordered behavior (Stein & Corte, 2003). Participants classified the behavior (e.g., vomiting, laxative use, binge eating) and answered questions about it. The results showed good compliance and a huge range in the number of disordered eating events: from five to 101.

- Wheeler and Nezlek (1977) asked college students to complete a survey about every social interaction—"any encounter of 10 minutes or longer with another person(s) in which the participants attended to one another and adjusted their behavior in response to one another" (p. 743)—during two 14-day periods. Among other things, they found that interactions were typically same-gender ones, but women had more frequent and longer other-gender interactions than men did.

- For 15 days, both members of a married couple completed a survey after each instance of marital conflict (Papp et al., 2009). They rated their emotions and described the conflict on several dimensions, most notably its topic (e.g., conflict over money, relatives, or chores, among others). An interesting finding was that money was only the fifth-most-common topic of conflict. Children, those infamous wreckers of household havoc, topped the list.

Researchers use event-based sampling when they don't want to miss any of the focal events. If your goal is to collect data about each and every single instance of the event—such as every time someone smokes a cigarette (e.g., Shiffman, 2009)—event-based sampling is the best design. You should consider using it when one of your animating research questions is "How often does X really happen?" or "How often do people actually do X?" If you ask participants to complete a brief survey every time they smoke a cigarette, for example, you'll get a solid estimate of how many times your participants smoked during the day. The estimate won't be perfect—participants will occasionally miss surveys—but event-based sampling will be as accurate as you can get with daily life methods (Himmelstein et al., 2019).

In addition to revealing how often an event happens, catching every instance of an event reveals its complexity and heterogeneity. Researchers seek to collect surveys on all instances when they expect the event to be diverse and variable. Social interactions, for example, are wide ranging: They involve partners and strangers, bosses and peers, friends and frenemies, parents and children, and they can be exciting, boring, frustrating, or disturbing, among many other emotions. If your study samples only the most recent or most memorable social interactions, it will tend to catch the most common kinds and miss the rare kinds. Likewise, if you expect that cigarette smoking has many situational and psychological triggers, not just a couple common ones, you should assess every instance of smoking to ensure that you catch the less prevalent triggers.

Event-based sampling works best for events that are *discrete, salient,* and *fairly frequent*. Discrete events have clear beginnings and endings—they usually did or didn't happen. Behaviors like smoking, drinking alcohol, waking from a nap, and talking with someone for at least 10 minutes are discrete events that can trigger people to complete a survey. Other events, in contrast, are "mushy," usually because they continuously ebb and flow throughout the day. Eating is discrete; feelings of hunger ebb and flow. Waking from sleep is discrete; subjective energy and fatigue are continuous. Getting into an argument with a relationship partner is discrete; irritation with your partner isn't. Discrete events with clear boundaries are good signals for participants to complete a survey; continuous, mushy events introduce biases from participants' own judgment about whether the focal event happened.

Salient events are easily noticed by participants, so event-based sampling is weaker for events that slip easily under the mental radar. People can experience events without being reflectively aware of the experience. The metacognitive awareness of conscious experience, known as *metaconsciousness* (Schooler, 2002), is necessary for an event to trigger a survey. When people get caught up in the flow of an event and don't reflectively label it as a focal event that triggers a survey, an event-based sampling design will miss many events and tend to catch only the most intense and salient ones. Subtle experiences are usually better sampled by interrupting people via random-interval sampling, which we describe later.

Finally, fairly frequent events fall into a sweet spot of not too rare and not too common. Event-based sampling fails when an event is too rare. Because participants complete a survey only when an event happens, you'll get no data when an event never happens to them. Imagine, for example, a 1-week study that asked people to complete a survey after every argument with a romantic partner. Many participants will have no arguments, so the study will have no responses—and hence 100% missing daily life data—from the participants with the happiest relationships. As a heuristic, you should expect an event to be common enough to happen to most participants during most days of the study and to happen to all participants at least a few times during the entire study. On the other side, an event can be too common. Imagine asking participants to fill out a survey after everything they eat or drink—every meal, snack, stick of gum, and sip from a water fountain. You'll get plenty of responses, but participants will get irritated by the incessant demands of the study. If the survey burden is too high, many participants will drop out, skip some surveys, or change their behavior (e.g., decide to stop snacking) to avoid completing yet another survey.

At the start of the study, the researcher must carefully define and describe the focal event to ensure a shared understanding (Moskowitz & Sadikaj, 2012). Even for a seemingly obvious event, you'll find that people define, interpret, and judge it differently. Smoking a cigarette seems straightforward, for example, but a few participants will think that one puff doesn't count, that second-hand smoke (sitting close to a friend who is smoking) doesn't count, or that using chewing tobacco or nicotine gum doesn't count. It's up to the researcher to define what counts and then ensure that everyone shares that definition (see Chapter 5).

FIXED-INTERVAL SAMPLING

Fixed-interval sampling, a time-based approach to sampling, signals people to provide data based on *when*. With this design, researchers ask people to complete surveys at times that don't change throughout the study—the intervals between surveys are fixed. Here are some good examples:

- For 2 weeks, people reported their negative emotions and borderline personality disorder (BPD) symptoms (e.g., feeling empty, avoiding abandonment) five times a day at fixed intervals (10:00 a.m., 1:00 p.m., 4:00 p.m., 7:00 p.m., and 10:00 p.m.). Higher negative affect predicted concurrent BPD symptoms for the sample overall, but negative affect and BPD symptoms were more tightly coupled for people with a BPD diagnosis (Law et al., 2016).

- A study of food and well-being asked a sample of 405 college-age adults to complete an end-of-day survey for 13 days (Conner et al., 2015). The survey asked about what people had eaten that day as well as their emotional experiences. On days when people ate relatively more fruit and vegetables, they experienced relatively higher positive affect, curiosity, and eudemonic well-being. (If you're wondering, french fries and potato chips didn't count as vegetables.)

- For 2 weeks, college students completed an end-of-day survey about their daily well-being and an array of daily activities and experiences (Reis et al., 2000). Consistent with self-determination theory, having a "good day" was strongly associated with daily experiences that satisfied needs for autonomy, competence, and relatedness.

This sampling design is also known as *interval-contingent sampling* because the prompt depends on a fixed time interval, like the passage of 2 hours. In practice, researchers tend to use one of two fixed-interval designs: *within-day designs*, which signal people several times a day, and *daily diary designs*, which signal people once a day.

Within-Day Fixed Intervals

Within-day interval designs are good for mapping what people are doing and thinking during the day. A typical design might ask people to complete a survey every 3 hours by beeping them with a text message, phone call, or smartphone notification. Some studies seek to catch the entire day, so the sampling would catch most of people's waking hours (e.g., signals every 4 hours throughout the day). Other studies seek to catch focal parts of the day, such as when people are at work (e.g., signals every 2 hours from 9:00 a.m. to 5:00 p.m.).

As we discuss in Chapter 3, questions in daily life surveys either ask about the present (what was happening when people were beeped), the past (what has happened since the last beep), or the future (what people expect to happen later in the day). It's almost always worth asking about what people are up to at the moment, but because this sampling design uses time intervals that are fixed and predictable, people with fixed, predictable schedules (e.g., always at their desk at 11:00 a.m.) will have the same responses to questions about what they're doing at the moment. As a result, researchers often ask questions that look back, such as whether people have smoked, exercised, or spent time with a friend since the last signal.

Sampling people every 3 or 4 hours and asking about what happened since the last signal is a good way to map what happens during a day. The events are close enough to remember well, but the number of surveys per day isn't so high that people get irritated and stop completing them. Recall biases, however, will creep in as the time window grows. People should easily recall everything they ate or drank in the past hour, for example, but their memories will slip if the time window stretches to 3, 4, or 6 hours.

The fixed, predictable signal times are both a strength and weakness of this sampling design. When people know that they will get beeped for a short survey every workday at 9:55 a.m. and 1:55 p.m. for 2 weeks, they will adjust to the interruption—they'll stop chatting with their coworkers in the halls and find a quiet place to reply to the survey. The good side is that people won't find the surveys intrusive, so compliance will be high and missing data will be low. The bad side, however, is that people will start rearranging their activities to fit the data collection. When the surveys become a predictable part of the daily routine, people will avoid scheduling certain kinds of events for those times. The surveys thus change the character of daily life, making it less random and variable during the survey times. This biasing effect is less troubling for "looking back" items (e.g., asking what people did in the past 4 hours) but could be a serious problem for "right now" items (e.g., asking what people were doing at the time of the signal).

Our impression is that within-day fixed-interval studies are less common than they used to be. In the past, researchers often used fixed times as a compromise with what the era's survey tools afforded, but advances in survey technology have made it easier to signal people at randomly varying times. Likewise, some statistical methods for within-person data (e.g., repeated-measures analysis of variance) require equally spaced time points, but the growth of advanced methods for analyzing intensive repeated measures has allowed more flexibility in signal times (see Chapter 7). Nevertheless, using fixed daily times for surveys remains a time-honored and practical way to map what happens throughout a day.

Daily Diaries

The daily diary method is the most popular kind of fixed-interval sampling and one of the cornerstone daily life designs (Gunthert & Wenze, 2012). In a daily diary design, participants are asked to complete a survey once per day. Instead of asking about momentary thoughts and feelings, these surveys ask about the day's events—they are thus a diary of the day, not a snapshot of a single point. Nearly all daily diary studies give the survey at night, which is why this design is sometimes called an *end-of-day* design. Participants are asked to complete the survey once the day has wound down, usually before they get ready for bed. Most daily diary questions ask about what people did, thought, and felt over the course of the day. In many cases, people are asked to select an event from the day, such as the most important goal they completed or their most stressful situation, and then answer some questions about it. Some surveys look ahead by asking questions about people's expectations and beliefs about the next day.

End-of-day diaries predominate, but a daily diary survey can be given anytime. For some research questions, daily diaries are completed on awakening. Studies of sleep, for example, often ask people about their sleep—duration, timing, quality, or dream experiences—when they wake up (e.g., Bertz et al., 2019; Soffer-Dudek & Shahar, 2011). Some studies collect morning diaries about the prior evening's behaviors, usually when the project is interested in behaviors that impair consistent and reliable end-of-day surveys (e.g., heavy drinking or risky sexual behavior; Muraven, Collins, Morsheimer, et al., 2005; Wray et al., 2016). A once-a-day survey may be linked to a milestone event that itself happens once a day. Researchers, for example, might give daily surveys to new teachers at the end of each school day, to office workers when they clock out, or to postsurgery outpatients after the day's physical therapy exercises.

Daily diaries are popular for good reasons. Humans, as diurnal creatures, wake up and go to sleep according to a daily rhythm, so days are the most intuitive and natural human unit of time (Landes, 2000; Palmer, 2002). Because days are natural psychological units, they are interesting in their own right. Many studies, for example, use daily diaries to show how people's moods and motivation vary during the week (e.g., differences between weekends and weekdays; Larsen & Kasimatis, 1990; Liu & West, 2016), how daily weather affects mood and energy (Denissen et al., 2008), and what makes "good days" good (Sheldon et al., 1996).

Daily diaries also hit a sweet spot of participant burden and study complexity, so they are good for studying people over long time periods. If your study requires only a 5-minute survey at the end of the day, participants would be willing to take part for weeks and weeks. The typical daily diary study is at least 10 days, usually 14 to 30 days, and occasionally 90 or more days (e.g., Lipton et al., 2014). You can learn a lot about someone's life if they describe what their days are like for several months. These designs are thus commonly used to look at things that stretch across many days, such as how artists make progress on complex, long-term creative projects (Benedek et al., 2017).

A final reason for the popularity of daily diaries, we suspect, is their simplicity. Compared with modern experience sampling, which uses increasingly expensive and specialized software and hardware, daily diary methods are cheap and low tech. A common approach, for example, is to set up an online survey, ask the participants to complete the survey on their own web-connected device each night, and send reminders via email. In a pinch, pencil-and-paper surveys are a respectable option for a daily diary study. Researchers curious to dip their toes into daily life methods should consider running a daily diary study before investing in the infrastructure for more complex studies.

Daily diary approaches are used for both highly frequent and infrequent behaviors. As we saw with event-based sampling, some events happen so often that it's impractical to ask participants to complete a survey after every instance. A compromise in those cases is to ask people about the collection of events once per day, such as an end-of-day survey that asks for a summary of how often people smoked, what they ate and drank, and what their social interactions were like. In some cases, the survey asks people to select a single event as an exemplar—such as the most stressful thing that happened or the most satisfying social interaction that they had—to describe in detail. Such an approach obviously provides less fine-grained detail than an event-based sampling design, but it allows researchers to collect data for many weeks.

Infrequent behaviors, in contrast, happen some days but not daily. Researchers must sample more often than the behavior happens for the typical participant (see Chapter 3). This means that daily diary studies work best when the main outcome varies across the days; most participants should report the outcome for at least some of the days. Consider, for example, a 14-day study interested in binge drinking. A daily diary design would work well if you expect the participants to have days where they binge drink and days where they don't. This allows you to compare, using within-person statistical methods, drinking days with dry days. But if many participants don't vary across the days—for each daily diary, they either never or always report binge drinking for that day—the daily diary design would be inapt.

When an event happens once a week or less, researchers use long daily diary designs to ensure enough of the events are sampled. For many health behaviors—such as using an asthma rescue inhaler, blacking out after drinking, or having a panic attack—even samples of higher risk participants might not have many episodes in a 14-day study. In a study of migraine headaches (Lipton et al., 2014), for example, adults recruited from a headache care center completed daily surveys about stress, sleep, and headaches for 12 weeks. Three months sounds like a long time to take part in a diary study, but the median number of headaches reported per participant was only five. Catching infrequent events like these requires long participation times, and short daily diaries are tolerable over long stretches.

The main drawback of daily diary designs is the potential for recall biases to creep in. In a typical study, people complete a retrospective survey about their day in the evening. The passage of time is thus one major source of bias. The day's events aren't far in the past, but 12 hours is a long time in a busy day. Many events are easy to remember and describe at the day's end, but many subtle and mundane events will have already been forgotten. When asked to recall and describe events, people's end-of-day judgments are likely to be swayed by events that are more recent, intense, and vivid (Schwartz, 2012). The physical and mental context is another source of bias. The days are diverse, but people are describing their days in similar places and mindsets. People typically complete end-of-day diaries in the same place (almost always their home) and the same frame of mind (a calm, tired, or frazzled evening mood). The effects of contexts and moods on memory are complex, but daily diary researchers suspect that people's judgments of their day are shaped by their evening environments and moods (Gunthert & Wenze, 2012). This drawback is part of the trade-off of daily diaries: The potential for recall bias is greater than for an event-based design, but daily diary studies can be carried out over long stretches of time.

RANDOM-INTERVAL SAMPLING

Random-interval sampling, like fixed-interval sampling, is a time-based approach to sampling—it beeps people to provide data based on *when*. With this design, however, researchers ask people to complete surveys at randomly selected, fluctuating times that change from day to day; the intervals between surveys are random. The random times nearly always vary within a day—signals pop up every 1 to 3 hours at random during the day for several days—but the intervals can be much longer or shorter (see Exhibit 2.1). It is an excellent way to study the fluid quality of someone's daily life. The following are a few examples of random schedules in the wild:

- College-age marijuana users were texted three times a day for 14 days and asked about their marijuana use, social context, academic motivation, and cravings (Phillips et al., 2014). The texts were sent at

---

EXHIBIT 2.1. Varieties of Random Intervals

The typical random-interval study is a within-day experience sampling study. People get signaled at quasi-random times throughout the day, usually once every couple of hours, and complete a brief survey about what is happening at the moment. But the intervals in a random-interval study can be much longer or shorter.

Some daily diary studies, for example, use long random intervals. Instead of asking participants to complete an end-of-day survey every day, these studies randomly select some days for surveys. Although uncommon, this design is used to reduce participant burden for unusually long studies that stretch across months. In a study of clinically depressed adults taking part in a psychotherapy trial, for example, the participants completed end-of-day diaries on two random days per week (Hoet et al., 2018). Because the psychotherapy trial took at least 4 months, sampling only two days per week allowed the researchers to sample for many months without undue hassle for participants. Like within-day sampling, such designs usually place some constraint on the random selection (e.g., the days can't be adjacent, or one day must be a weekend day).

Other random-interval studies, in contrast, sample frequently from a small portion of the day. These designs are used in studies with durations measured in minutes or hours instead of days. The overall experience being sampled is shorter (e.g., a few hours spent in a museum; Smith, 2014), but the logic of random sampling is the same. Participants are less likely to adapt their actions to accommodate unpredictable surveys, and interrupting participants is more likely to reveal fleeting and subtle experiences.

random times within morning (8:00 a.m.–12:00 p.m.), afternoon (12:30 p.m.–4:30 p.m.), and evening (5:00 p.m.–10:00 p.m.) time blocks but were adapted to participants' course schedules to avoid texting them during class.

- For 6 days, adults were called five times daily at quasi-random times to complete a survey using an interactive voice response system (see Chapter 4). They answered questions about whether they were working on a creative project as well as about their emotional state and social activity (Karwowski et al., 2017). Doing something creative was associated with activated positive emotions.

- For a single workday, adults completed brief surveys about their momentary emotions and social behaviors three times an hour, at random intervals within each hour, for a full waking day (Smart Richman et al., 2010). These surveys were linked to concurrent blood pressure readings to illuminate relationships among a history of discrimination, daily mood and stressors, and cardiovascular activity.

Researchers use random-interval sampling when they want to describe what people are doing, thinking, and feeling throughout the day. Of the designs, this one is the most analogous to randomly sampling people from a population; by beeping at random, researchers get a representative sampling of the participants' daily experience. This sampling design is commonly known as *signal-contingent sampling* because the survey is contingent on receiving a signal, not on an event happening (event based) or on the passage of a time period (fixed interval). The most common label is probably *experience sampling*, a term that reflects this design's historical origins in studying people's momentary thoughts and emotions (Hektner et al., 2007).

Random-interval sampling is never truly random. Randomness in sampling, as in many other areas of life, is too random to be practical. For example, researchers don't randomly assign participants to an experimental condition by flipping a coin because, according to probability theory, sometimes almost everyone will end up in one condition. Likewise, if you set an experience-sampling program to signal people randomly 10 times a day, occasionally participants would get all 10 beeps within an hour. You wouldn't learn much about that day, and the participants would be muttering unseemly words.

Instead, random-interval studies break the day into bins of time. If you want to sample between 8:00 a.m. and midnight, for example, you can split the 16 hours into eight blocks of 120 minutes. The software that signals participants can be set to beep them at a random time once per block. This ensures that each part of the day gets captured and injects enough randomness to prevent participants from anticipating and preparing for signals. But a quirk of using blocks is that someone will, by chance, occasionally get beeped at the end of one block (e.g., 1:58 p.m.) and the start of the next one (e.g., 2:04 p.m.). This grates on participants and yields patchy coverage of the day. To prevent this, most software allows you to specify a minimum time between beeps (e.g., beeps must be at least 20 minutes apart). When we discuss "random sampling" throughout this book, we're referring to this kind of constrained, quasi-random sampling structure.

The difference between sampling according to fixed versus random time intervals may seem small, but these designs get used for different purposes and have different strengths. Consider, for example, a 10-day fixed-interval study that beeps participants five times daily every 3 hours at five fixed times (e.g., 10:00 a.m., 1:00 p.m., 4:00 p.m., 7:00 p.m., and 10:00 p.m.) versus a random-interval study that also beeps people five times daily but does so at a random point within ± 45 minutes of those five times. For the fixed-time study, participants will start to anticipate the surveys, causing them to reshuffle activities and avoid distractions around the time of the survey. For the random-time study, participants will go about their day normally because they expect to be beeped any time. In the first case, surveys feel like an upcoming task; in the second, they feel like an unexpected interruption. Compared with fixed-interval schedules, random-interval sampling feels more disruptive to daily life, but participants are less likely to adapt their actions to it.

Second, the regularity of the fixed times can parallel regularities in participants' daily routines. Because of work, school, and habit, an adult's weekdays are reasonably similar from day to day. For the fixed signal times at 10:00 a.m. and 4:00 p.m., for example, you will be tapping into the sorts of things your participants tend to do at 10:00 a.m. and 4:00 p.m. every day. Shifting the surveys by even 20 minutes in either direction will likely yield different activities. Fixed-interval sampling tends to underestimate the day-to-day variability in people's experience; random-interval sampling is more representative.

Third, the survey questions tend to differ. Fixed-interval surveys are often used to ask about what has happened in the recent past, such as the hour prior to the beep. Random-interval surveys, in contrast, almost always focus on the present—what people were doing, thinking, and feeling when they were interrupted by the beep. When survey times are fixed and evenly spaced, using past signals as milestones is sensible; when the survey times are unevenly spaced throughout the day, it makes less sense to use past beeps as benchmarks. For example, answers to the question "Have you smoked a cigarette since the last survey?" aren't strictly comparable in a random-interval study because the time gap between surveys could be anywhere between 30 minutes and 2 hours, depending on the signal design. For this reason, random-interval designs emphasize immediate experience and the near past (e.g., framing items in terms of "the past 10 minutes"; see Chapter 3).

Random-interval designs have many strengths. Because this design takes random slices from a day, it is a great way to describe what a person's day was like. This approach is ideal for measuring what people are doing at the moment: where they are, who is around them, and what they are thinking about and experiencing. The design's popularity among emotion researchers and health scientists attests to its usefulness for catching inner states that ebb and flow throughout the day, such as emotions, fatigue, pain, clinical symptoms, and other subjective experiences.

Random signaling is ideal for fleeting events that people don't notice. For event-based sampling, we discussed how some events don't enter meta-consciousness. When people are daydreaming, for example, they aren't always meta-cognitively aware that they are daydreaming, so they won't consistently catch themselves doing it. When researchers are interested in such subtle experiences, they are better off randomly interrupting the participants and asking what they were thinking and feeling when beeped. Participants no longer need to monitor their experiences for focal events or remember to do surveys when an event happens.

Because random-interval sampling gives a reasonably representative snapshot of a person's day, it allows researchers to discern psychological patterns and relationships that participants might not notice themselves. For example, if we assess people's momentary emotional states and their social behaviors dozens of times across a typical week, we can estimate the relationship between emotional states and social behavior, ranging from general effects (e.g., social interaction is associated with positive affect; Watson, 2000) to more subtle and qualified effects (e.g., social anhedonia moderates the effect of social contact on positive affect; Kwapil et al., 2009). Similarly, people lack insight into many diurnal trends (Palmer, 2002), but these trends are obvious when you sample across the day (e.g., Peeters et al., 2006; Watson, 2000).

Like all the designs, random-interval sampling has its drawbacks. First, it is the most technically intricate and hence expensive method of signaling people. Researchers have many technology options (see Chapter 4), but any system capable of sending constrained random signals is usually relatively expensive compared with daily diaries and event-based surveys. Aside from the cost of buying and using the system, researchers will spend more time and money on training research staff, monitoring the system for quirks and crashes, and troubleshooting the inevitable tech problems.

Second, random-interval designs have higher participant burden. Because the beeps are random, the participants are continually interrupted during their day to fill out surveys. In later chapters, we describe ways of reducing and balancing the hassle of experience sampling surveys. This hassle is the trade-off for the benefits of random sampling. Some things are best studied by randomly interrupting people, but people get irritated if the surveys are too long or too frequent.

Third, random-interval studies will miss a lot of focal events. They will give a reasonably representative snapshot of the day, but many events happen between the beeps. If you want a precise estimate of how often something happens, such as how often your participants smoke a cigarette or commit a self-harming act, an event-based approach will catch more events and thus give a more accurate frequency estimate.

Fourth, sometimes you are interested in something that doesn't lend itself well to interruption. Researchers hope that the participants will always stop what they're doing to fill out a survey, but people simply won't halt some events. For example, it would be nice to sample musicians' thoughts and experiences while rehearsing, but accomplished musicians are reluctant to interrupt their deep, focused practice to complete a survey. In many contexts, such as while teaching a class or attending a classical music concert, stopping and filling out a survey would be socially inappropriate. Sometimes, completing the survey would be unsafe and possibly illegal, such as when people are operating planes, trains, and automobiles. Sampling designs that look back, such as event-based designs or daily diaries, are better suited to such events.

And finally, a relatively minor limitation is the uneven spacing of the signals. When researchers are interested in temporal trends (e.g., estimating the shape of a curve across a day) or in estimates of variability and volatility (Jahng et al., 2008), evenly spaced assessment points are simpler to work with statistically (see Chapter 7).

ALL OF THE ABOVE: COMBINING SAMPLING DESIGNS

The three designs we've described—event-based, fixed-interval, and random-interval sampling—are prototypical, classic designs (see Exhibit 2.2). Most research projects use only one sampling approach, but it's common for a

EXHIBIT 2.2. A Look at Active Versus Passive Sampling Strategies

A dimension of sampling we haven't discussed is whether data collection is *active* or *passive* (Conner & Lehman, 2012). Active sampling is when the participant must deliberately engage with the study to provide data. Completing self-report questions—the focus of this book—is the most common instance; collecting a saliva sample and snapping a picture of your location are other examples of active sampling.

Passive sampling, in contrast, requires no involvement from the participants: The data roll in without their input and often without their knowledge that, at that moment, their day is being sampled. Passive sampling usually focuses on environmental features (e.g., ambient noise, Global Positioning System [GPS] location) or physiological features (e.g., respiration, heart rate, and skin temperature). Passive data collection follows the same sampling strategies.

- **Event based.** Sensors in a device can trigger passive data collection (Miller, 2012). For example, on the basis of changes in activity level or GPS location, a device could take a snapshot, collect cardiac readings, or measure ambient light and sound.

- **Fixed interval.** A digital device can be set to collect data snippets at fixed intervals, such as recording 30 seconds of sound every 18 minutes (Bollich et al., 2016).

- **Random interval.** A device can be set to collect data at quasi-random times, such as programming an ambulatory blood pressure monitor to inflate at random intervals three times per hour to take cardiovascular readings (Smart Richman et al., 2010).

Passive sampling affords a new, fourth sampling design: *continuous sampling*. This design collects data second by second throughout the day, such as continuous physiological monitoring (e.g., heart rate sampled at 500 Hz via an ambulatory electrocardiogram monitor) or environmental sensing (e.g., noise exposure).

---

project to combine designs into different layers. With some planning, you can mix and match daily life designs in ways that combine their strengths.

A common mash-up is adding a daily diary study to an experience sampling study. For the experience sampling layer, participants are randomly signaled throughout the day to ask about momentary experiences. For the daily diary layer, a study could add a morning diary that assesses when people woke up and their sleep quality (e.g., Bouwmans et al., 2017). More often, a study would add an end-of-day diary that asks about global features of the day to complement the random sampling (e.g., Muraven, Collins, Shiffman, & Paty, 2005). Some studies add both morning and evening diaries to a within-day experience sampling design (e.g., Hamilton et al., 2008).

Another combination is adding event-based surveys to an experience sampling study. As we discussed earlier, a limitation of random-interval designs is that they miss a lot of events. If you want a broad sample of people's experiences and an accurate count of a focal event, you can create an experience sampling study that both randomly interrupts participants and allows them to initiate a survey when the focal event happens. Some studies of nonsuicidal self-injury, for example, not only randomly prompt people during the day to ask about such episodes but also have them initiate a survey after one (e.g., Armey et al., 2011). Combining an end-of-day diary with an event-based study allows researchers to see how the day's events—how often the focal event happened, if at all—predict global features of the day and to catch focal events that people didn't flag during the day (e.g., Shiffman, 2009).

Finally, you can use similar time-based designs at different time scales. A randomized trial that compared two psychotherapies for depression, for example, used three sampling designs to evaluate how people's symptoms changed across the months of treatment: (a) fixed-interval sampling of depressive symptoms via weekly symptom surveys (Eddington et al., 2015), (b) random-interval sampling of end-of-day surveys (two randomly picked days per week) that asked about how people were using the skills they were learning (Hoet et al., 2018), and (c) random-interval experience sampling (eight signals daily for 7 days) for the week before and week after treatment to assess changes in momentary thoughts and emotions (Eddington et al., 2017). Combining designs allows you to look at your research question at different time scales and levels of detail.

CONCLUSION

In this chapter, we have described two broad approaches to sampling from daily life: sampling based on *events* and on *time*. These two sampling strategies afford many options for creatively capturing the complexity of daily experience. Like all research designs, the sampling designs described in this chapter have strengths and limitations, and understanding these trade-offs is key to selecting the design that is right for your research. Now that we understand our options for sampling from daily life, what do we ask when we sample? What do daily life surveys look like? In the next chapter, we describe how to design good self-report questions for daily life studies.

3 DESIGNING SELF-REPORT SURVEYS

Stripped down to its basics, self-report daily life research involves two things: signaling people in their real-world environment and giving them a survey. In Chapter 2, we reviewed *sampling designs,* which are frameworks for deciding when to signal people. In this chapter, we discuss the second part—how to design and give daily life surveys. Even though daily life research explores most of the same affective, cognitive, and behavioral constructs as lab and survey research, the self-report scales used in cross-sectional projects can rarely be transplanted as is to a daily life study.

Compared with conventional surveys—like personality inventories, stressful life-events checklists, and attitude scales—daily life surveys have four interesting features:

1. **Repetition:** People complete the same items over and over again, often dozens or even hundreds of times.

2. **Compression:** The surveys and their items are as short and focused as possible, both to save time and render well on small screens.

https://doi.org/10.1037/0000236-003
Researching Daily Life: A Guide to Experience Sampling and Daily Diary Methods,
by P. J. Silvia and K. N. Cotter
Copyright © 2021 by the American Psychological Association. All rights reserved.

3. **Time reference:** Instead of asking for typical experiences, the items refer to specific times, such as participants' experiences right now, since the past survey, or over the past day.
4. **Context coverage:** The items' meaning must make sense not merely in general but in the specific and eclectic contexts that participants are in.

With these factors in mind, we'll describe how to make an *assessment design*—a framework for the frequency and length of the daily life assessment—and how to craft self-report questions that work well in daily life contexts.

THE TRADE-OFFS AMONG ITEMS, BEEPS, AND DAYS

The first decision to make is your assessment design—the abstract structure of your daily life assessment. You'll need to nail down three factors: *days*, *beeps*, and *items*.

- For *days*, how many days do you want to assess? For how many days will people take part? Will your study be an intensive, single-day study stuffed with surveys (e.g., Sperry et al., 2018)? A 7-day experience sampling study (Granholm et al., 2020)? Perhaps a study that collects daily surveys for as long as 1, 2, or 3 months (Lipton et al., 2014)?

- For *beeps*, how often will you signal people per day? Once per day, as in a prototypical daily diary study? Twice per day, perhaps with surveys upon waking and before bed (e.g., Lipton et al., 2014)? Once every 6, 4, or 2 hours? Every 15 minutes?

- And for *items*, how many items will you ask at each signal? Perhaps 50 at the end of the day? A focused set of 30, 20, or 10 items during the day? Only one item (Intille et al., 2016)?

Choosing the right balance of days, signals, and items is crucial for a successful daily life study (Eisele et al., 2020). A newcomer to daily life research might want to have as many of everything as possible—a 2-month study that asks 40 questions eight times a day. In theory, that design would yield a large, rich data set. But in practice, it would be a morass of slow recruitment, low participant compliance, and high dropout. Unless your incentives to participate are enormous, the participants' engagement with your study will suffer when the survey burden is too high.

The craft of daily life assessment is creating an assessment design that optimally balances data density and participant burden. Days, beeps, and items tug against each other and thus represent a series of trade-offs that researchers must make thoughtfully (Cotter & Silvia, 2019; Eisele et al., 2020; Silvia et al., 2014). The first trade-off is *days versus beeps*. People will take part for more days if there are fewer beeps per day. Holding survey length constant, you can have a lot of beeps per day for a few days (e.g., 15 signals a day for 2 days), and you can have a few beeps per day for a lot of days (e.g., two signals a day for 60 days)—but you can't have a lot of beeps per day for a lot of days.

The second trade-off is *beeps versus items*. If you ask people to complete a survey many times a day, the survey must be short; if you give people only one survey per day, it can be long. Later we describe how to reduce the duration of your survey, but the number of items is the main factor. No one wants to fill out a 60-item survey about their thoughts and feelings every 45 minutes, but people would do a long survey once a day in the evening. Likewise, if your survey is only a few items, people would be willing to fill it out a dozen times a day.

Designing the assessment plan for a daily life study is thus a classic optimality problem. Researchers must balance the desire for data quantity with the usual constraints—time, money, and personnel—as well as the constraint of participant patience and goodwill. We encourage researchers who are new to daily life methods to use the time-honored principle of "adopting best practices," which is a scholarly euphemism for "following the herd" and "imitating the popular kids." Search the literature for published studies with participant populations like yours and take note of their assessment designs and compliance rates (the proportion of surveys that were completed; see Chapter 5). Past work will provide excellent guidance for the range of days, signals, and items that your sample would accept.

You don't want to overwhelm your participants with surveys, but you shouldn't underwhelm them either. For reasons we go into later (see Chapter 6), it's rarely worth doing a daily life study if you don't expect to get at least five completed surveys per person (Bolger & Laurenceau, 2013), and five is a small minimum for describing someone's daily life and estimating within-person statistical relationships. You can forecast the expected number of completed surveys per participant by multiplying days, signals, and compliance:

Expected surveys per participant =

Days in the study × Signals per day × Expected compliance rate

The "compliance rate" term adjusts your results to account for missing data—participants won't complete all the surveys, so simply multiplying days and signals will overstate how many responses your design will yield. Compliance is complex, but we'll use a 65% survey completion rate—a realistic value in experience sampling and daily diary studies—for the sake of example.

If you want to conduct a daily diary study with one end-of-day survey, a seven-day study would be too sparse ($7 \times 1 \times .65 \approx 4.5$ surveys per participant), a 10-day study would be barely adequate ($10 \times 1 \times .65 \approx 6.5$ surveys per participant), 14 would be reasonable (9.1 surveys), and at least 21 days would be ideal. It isn't a coincidence that the typical daily diary study lasts at least 2 weeks. Likewise, if you want to conduct a random-interval experience sampling study with six surveys per day, one day isn't enough ($1 \times 6 \times .65 \approx 3.9$ surveys per participant), three days is solid ($3 \times 6 \times .65 \approx 11.7$ surveys per participant), and 7 days—a common number in published work—is great (27.3 surveys).

This simple formula implies two ways to increase your data yield. The first way involves your project's design—you can add days, add more surveys per day, or both. The second way involves your procedures and practices—you can invest in research practices that increase response rates (see Chapter 5), such as incentives, reminders, and alliance.

DEVELOPING ITEMS

Newcomers to daily life research usually have a focal construct they want to study, often the construct they have been studying with lab and survey methods, and are excited to explore in the real world. A common beginner's intuition is that a popular scale in cross-sectional studies can be used, with some tweaks and nips and tucks, in a daily life study, thereby bridging the two literatures. But most scales used in survey research—even gold-standard scales, and often especially those—can't be squeezed into a daily life project. We can take inspiration, ideas, and occasionally items from those scales, but it is better to develop daily life items from the ground up.

Why won't traditional surveys work? We'll cover two reasons: They are too long, and their item content is too abstract to apply to daily experience.

Length

Traditional self-report scales used in survey research are usually too long to work as is in daily life studies. Those scales were designed for cross-sectional studies, and their developers usually sought to increase internal-consistency reliability by adding items (DeVellis, 2017). Consider extraversion, a complex construct made of up features like gregariousness (being outgoing and socially bold) and positive affectivity (feeling energetic and enthusiastic; Wilt & Revelle, 2009). Personality psychologists have many self-report scales for assessing extraversion, but they're long: 48 items in the NEO Personality Inventory-3 (McCrae et al., 2005), 20 items in the Big Five Aspects Scale (DeYoung et al., 2007), and 16 items in the HEXACO-100 (Lee & Ashton, 2018).

Assuming that their items would even make sense in daily life, these scales are impractical for daily life studies. In an intensive within-day experience sampling study, for example, 20 items would take up most of the 30 items that you could reasonably expect participants to do.

The length of a daily life survey is captured by two metrics: the *number of items* (e.g., 20 items per signal) and *duration* to complete (e.g., it takes 100 seconds, on average, to complete the survey). These metrics are obviously related—the number of items is the single biggest contributor to duration—but they are different targets for trimming a survey. Here are some strategies for reducing survey length that focus on each metric.

Reducing the Number of Items

Imagine an intensive experience sampling study that measures these constructs: nicotine cravings, positive affect, negative affect, nicotine use in the past hour, cognitive clarity, and social interaction. The researchers plan to ask 20 items per signal, but their first survey draft has 24 items. It's time for the scalpel, but which items should get sliced off?

When trimming a survey, consider the distinction between removing *items* and removing *constructs*. In our example, perhaps "cognitive clarity" is measured with four items. The researchers could shrink their survey by lopping off this construct and keeping the rest of the items. Instead, they could keep all the constructs and shave one item from four different constructs. The tension is between scope and measurement quality: measuring more constructs with fewer items versus measuring fewer constructs with more items. Although there's no easy answer to such trade-offs, there's something to be said for leaning toward scope. Measuring more constructs expands the number of hypotheses you can explore—you get more scholarly bang for your research bucks (see Exhibit 3.1).

Thinning items becomes easier once you learn to befriend short scales—even single items. This can be hard at first. Many researchers were raised in earlier times, with its skepticism of short scales and confusion of Cronbach's

EXHIBIT 3.1. Thinking in Papers

Daily life projects are more like longitudinal projects in developmental psychology than laboratory experiments in social and cognitive psychology. Longitudinal studies explore many scientific questions using a single sample; lab experiments, in contrast, usually test one big idea per sample. As a result, longitudinal studies yield many papers per sample, but lab experiments often yield many samples per paper.

Daily life studies afford the collection of an enormous amount of data from a sample of people. With some foresight, you can craft the design to generate more than one publication, thus yielding more scholarly knowledge for everyone's time and trouble. When planning your survey, then, consider expanding the number of constructs instead of expanding the number of items per construct. Adding an interesting construct, even with only one item, will enlarge the scientific scope of your work.

Note that we're not encouraging a "least publishable unit" approach to research (see Silvia, 2015, for a condemnation of such nonsense). Instead, everyone has limited time and resources available for research, especially for complex daily life studies, and we should be good stewards of the research resources that our institutions and funding agencies provide. Perhaps the most precious resource is our participants' time, motivation, and goodwill. Research ethics requires us to balance the hassles and risks experienced by our participants with the eventual contribution to scholarly knowledge. We owe it to our participants to learn as much as possible from their irksome weeks of being pestered with surveys.

---

alpha with reliability (Henson, 2001; McNeish, 2018). The number of items is only one psychometric facet in an assessment design (Brennan, 2001; Linacre, 1994). Daily life studies have fewer items but many more occasions. Asking people to complete a two-item fatigue scale 50 times should yield more reliable scores than asking them to complete a 10-item scale once, all else equal. To return to our extraversion example, experience sampling studies have measured this trait with only a handful of items (e.g., "talkative," "adventurous," "energetic," and "assertive"; Fleeson, 2001). Four items might not seem like much, but reliability is a function of the full assessment design: four items assessed five times daily for 13 days, in Fleeson's (2001) study, which is a lot of scores.

Many aspects of daily life are routinely measured with only one or two items. For some variables, using more than one item would seem weird—there are only so many ways to ask someone if they have used nicotine in the past hour or if they are listening to music right now. But even for more complex constructs, you can go far with only one or two items that target a construct's core features and make sense in people's diverse daily environments. In an ideal world, for example, an experience sampling study would have a well-rounded assessment of emotional states, but in a pinch you can learn a lot from just a single item about happiness (Schimmack, 2003).

Speeding Up a Survey

The number of items is the single biggest cause of survey duration, but there are ways to speed up a survey without shaving off items. Exhibit 3.2 lists some common predictors of survey duration along with some tips for making a survey faster. We offer this list as food for thought, not as a recommendation to use every tool. Some ways of speeding up a survey are usually worth doing if they are feasible: Writing crisp, short items, for example, is always important, and formatting items as matrix tables will foster both speed and participant comprehension.

But other features that speed up a survey can degrade data quality, so faster is not always better. For example, randomizing items within a block—such as presenting 10 emotion items in a different order at each beep—is a good practice for surveys. After seeing a survey over and over, participants will habituate to the predictable item order and may start responding habitually. Shuffling items within a block disrupts automatic skimming of the survey and thus slows down participants, but trading time for data quality is a trade worth making.

A Time and a Place

The second reason why traditional self-report scales work poorly for daily life is that the scales weren't designed to make sense in the contexts and time frames that daily life researchers want to understand. People's environments are eclectic, quirky, and singular, so most self-report scales would strike participants as confusing and weird if transported to a daily life survey.

To see why, let's look at some kinds of survey items for measuring abstract qualities outside of specific contexts. Curiosity, for example, is interesting both to personality psychologists, who study it as a stable, transsituational quality of people (Silvia & Kashdan, 2017), and to daily life researchers, who study how it varies within and across days (e.g., Conner et al., 2015; Kashdan & Steger, 2007). Trait curiosity scales used in personality research usually ask people to describe global self-beliefs, such as "I am the type of person who really enjoys the uncertainty of everyday life" (Kashdan et al., 2009). Such statements transcend too many situations to be useful in studying enjoyment of uncertainty in any particular time and place. Other curiosity items ask about general qualities of one's life, such as "My spare time is filled with interesting activities" (Naylor, 1981), instead of specific qualities of the past hour or past day. Some items ask about typical behaviors, often quite specific or eccentric ones, such as "When I see a new fabric, I like to touch and feel it" (Collins et al., 2004). Your participants might love

EXHIBIT 3.2. Surveying, Fast and Slow

The number of items is the biggest predictor of survey duration, but researchers can control a few other factors when designing their surveys.

- **Item length.** The items should be as short and compressed as possible. Longer, wordier items are rarely better. The timeless virtue of "omit needless words" aside (Strunk & White, 2000, p. 23), short items will display better on cramped smartphone screens.
- **Item complexity.** Some items are harder to answer because they require a more complex judgment ("Are you alone?" vs. "How many people are within 50 feet of you right now?") or require recalling more information ("Did you take a nap today?" vs. "How many minutes did you nap during the day?").
- **Item presentation.** Your participants will either read or hear your items. For literate samples, reading is usually faster than listening. For systems that speak items aloud, such as interactive voice response systems (Chapter 4), researchers can choose to allow participants to respond while the item is being spoken, which is faster, or force them to wait until the item has finished playing, which ensures they know what item they are responding to.
- **Response capture.** Most methods capture responses via tapping a screen, typing on a keyboard, speaking aloud, or writing on paper. For some item types, such as long, open-ended responses, people can usually speak aloud the response much faster than they can type it, especially on a small device.
- **Going back.** Some systems allow participants to go back to earlier items and change their responses. Participants rarely do so, but we suspect that the option slows down indecisive and perfectionistic people.
- **Confirming responses.** Some systems require (or give researchers the option to require) participants to confirm their responses. After tapping "Strongly Agree" as an item response, for example, the participant would have to additionally tap "Confirm" or "Next" to move to the next item. Doubling the number of taps greatly slows down participants and gets on their nerves; on the other hand, it reduces errors caused by inattentiveness and "fat fingers" on small screens. If participants can't go back to correct a mistake, confirming responses probably gains more in data quality than it loses in survey time.
- **Items per screen.** Some systems allow you to present several items on the screen at once, such as a matrix table. For example, a group of emotion items might start with a shared stem ("Right now, I feel . . .") and a group of items ("happy," "sad," "excited," "irritated"). Other systems present only a single item at a time. Matrix tables for related items are much faster than item-by-item presentation.
- **Randomization.** Randomizing the order of items within a block—such as displaying 10 emotion items in a different order each beep—prevents participants from habituating to an order and responding thoughtlessly. Randomizing items thus slows them down, by requiring more attention to reading, but improves data quality.
- **Subsetting.** The typical study presents all survey items at all occasions. You can, however, present subsets of items using efficient design principles from missing data theory (Silvia et al., 2014). For a five-item positive affect scale, for example, you can present random subsets of two or three items. This is an advanced method for reducing the number of items per occasion without reducing the number of items overall, so researchers should avoid wading into it without thoughtful planning.

fondling textiles more than most people, but the item is inapt for those days when they don't encounter an intriguing chambray. Finally, many items ask about hypothetical situations that reveal people's self-theories, such as "I would like to take off on a trip with no preplanned routes or timetables" (Hoyle et al., 2002). Hypothetical items are ill suited to assessing what people actually do in the real world.

In short, trait surveys aim to capture something that transcends specific times and places, but daily life surveys want to capture those times and places. As a result, a cardinal feature of daily life items is *time referencing*. Time-referenced items ask participants to respond according to a point on the stream of time: the past, present, or future. Daily life items should have an obvious time anchor that makes sense for your construct so that all participants understand the item similarly.

Past

Most studies ask questions about the past, a slippery creature. When you anchor an event in the past, you are using either *clock time* or *event time* as a reference point. Clock time uses quantitative anchors:

- Did you exercise during the last 4 hours?
- In the past hour, how many cigarettes have you smoked?
- Since noon, how many caffeinated drinks have you had?

Event time uses behavioral or environmental landmarks as anchors:

- Since waking up this morning, how many cigarettes have you smoked?
- Did you have a stressful interaction during work hours today?
- During your last class, did you use your smartphone for activities unrelated to the class?
- Since returning home from work, did you hug or kiss your relationship partner?

Think through what "the past" could mean for an item to ensure that you and your participants agree. For clock-time anchors, be specific about your time frame. It is better, for example, to ask "Have you smoked a cigarette in the past 10 minutes?" than "Have you recently smoked a cigarette?" For other anchors, avoid uninformed assumptions about what the participants' days are like. The typical daily diary study, for example, asks people to complete an end-of-day survey about their day, but when does a day start? An implicit anchor is waking time—the time window starts with when people woke up and got out of bed. But when your sample has a subset of people with nontraditional sleep, such as people working night shifts, new parents with volatile sleep patterns, college students staying up all night, or teens who sleep in until the midafternoon, they might not share your implicit definition of when the day started. These issues should be handled during the initial orientation instructions to the participants, where you define an item's meaning and answer questions about the survey (see Chapter 5).

Finally, we discourage using the survey signals as time anchors. In a within-day experience sampling study, for example, one could ask, "Since the last beep, have you smoked a cigarette?" This is straightforward only when everyone notices and responds to every signal. But some participants might have skipped the last survey, perhaps because they were napping or driving. When completing the item, some will think "the last beep" means "the last beep I heard," and others will think it means "the last beep I responded to." A further wrinkle is when participants don't notice a beep, such as when the environment is noisy or their device is silenced, making "since the last beep" an ambiguous anchor. It's better to use a specific clock time ("in the last 60 minutes") or event time ("since you arrived at work") instead of signals as an anchor.

Present

Your items might concern what is happening in the present. Most within-day experience sampling studies, for example, are curious about what is happening "right now": where people are, who they are with, and what they are doing and thinking. But what time is now? Without clear instructions and training, participants will understand items about the present differently. An item like "Right now, I feel irritated" can mean a couple things to participants:

- "At the time of the signal, right before I was interrupted around 20 seconds ago, I felt irritated."

- "Right now, as I'm completing this cursed survey for the 40th time this week, I feel irritated."

It is a natural misunderstanding, but experience samplers nearly always want to know about what was happening at the time of the beep—to them, "right now" means "around 20 seconds ago, right before we interrupted you." For items focused on the present moment, you should explain what you mean by "right now" during your participant orientation session (see Chapter 5).

When presenting your items in the survey, consider including a reminder of the time frame in your item stem. A series of emotion items, for example, can be delivered with a shared item stem: "Right now, I feel . . ." or "At the time of the beep, my mood was . . ." followed by affect items (e.g., "happy," "sad," "irritated"). Surveys often mix time references—most items might be about the present, but a few might be about the past hour or the day thus far—so clearly anchoring each item's time reference reduces confusion.

Future

Items about the future allow researchers to explore what their participants plan to do and expect to happen:

- How many cigarettes, if any, do you expect to smoke in the next 2 hours?
- Do you plan to exercise in the next 4 hours?
- How stressful do you think tomorrow's day at work will be?

Items like these are useful for understanding the beliefs that shape people's choices and for illuminating people's insight into their own future behavior.

An interesting use of future items is to assess expected responding. In a daily diary study, one might ask, "How likely are you to complete tomorrow's end-of-day survey?" followed up with "Why?" when people expect to skip it. In a random-interval experience sampling study, one might ask, "The next survey is roughly 90 to 120 minutes away. Do you expect to complete it?" Daily life studies have complex patterns of missingness (see Chapter 6), so understanding at least some of the reasons why people miss surveys can clarify threats to validity posed by missing data. In addition, having a predictor of missingness can also sharpen your statistical models. As research on missing data shows, tools for estimating effects that account for missing data are more effective when you have predictors of a score's absence (Enders, 2010).

Don't Reinvent the Wheel

When designing your survey, don't reinvent the wheel. By this point, there are dozens of research labs that have being doing daily life research for decades and have plenty of good wheels laying around. Search for items that have stood the test of time and peer review before writing new ones. Many researchers have published their survey items in tables, appendixes, or online materials; you should, too, to save someone else some time and trouble (see Chapter 8).

One modern trend is the development of standard scales that researchers can plug into projects. Most of this work is done in clinical and health contexts, which have been faster to appreciate the value of standard scales in fostering a cumulative literature. When many researchers are studying similar populations and symptoms, using the same daily life scales makes their studies more comparable and the literature more easily synthesized. Daily life versions of patient-reported outcomes, for example, show great promise for bridging cross-sectional studies and daily life studies (Carlson et al., 2016; Schneider et al., 2013; Schneider & Stone, 2016).

Once you have a good wheel, either invented or borrowed, you should reuse it. Your own program of research will be more cumulative when you include some of the same items in each study, such as the same items measuring mood or social activity. With shared items, your data sets can be linked and pooled, thus allowing you to combine them to answer new questions that no single study was equipped to answer.

SURVEY FEATURES

Now that you have your items, how should you assemble them into a survey? Although you can tinker endlessly with surveys, three big design decisions stand out: selecting which items go first, defining conditional branching, and choosing whether to randomize the items.

What Goes First?

For most surveys, the pivotal items should go first. In experience sampling studies with a focal event in mind—such as whether people were mind-wandering (Kane et al., 2007), smoking (Garrison et al., 2020), doing something creative (Karwowski et al., 2017), or hearing music in their mind (Cotter et al., 2019)—you should ask about the focal event early in the survey. The point of interrupting people is to catch them during events they might not otherwise notice, so ask about the most central constructs before people's impressions and experiences fade. Items about secondary constructs and items requiring less introspection to answer—such as where people are and who they are with—can be asked later in the survey.

Branching

Most survey tools afford *conditional branching* to different sets of items based on a response. If a survey asks whether people are alone at the moment, for example, responding "no" can branch to questions about the social interaction (e.g., who they are with and if the interaction is pleasant), and responding "yes" can branch to questions about solitude (e.g., if they are alone by choice and if they would rather be with other people; e.g., Kwapil et al., 2009). In other cases, only one branch includes items. A study on eating behavior, for example, could ask if people have had anything to drink in the past 60 minutes. People who responded "yes" would get asked for details with follow-up questions, which would be skipped for participants who responded "no."

Branching can make a survey much shorter or longer as a result of participants' responses. For a one-shot, cross-sectional survey it's rarely a big deal if a survey is 30% longer for some people. But for daily life studies, where participants take the same survey dozens of times, different survey lengths can cause compliance problems. Consider, for example, a study of eating that asks five main items followed by "Have you had anything to eat or drink in the past 30 minutes?" If people respond "no," the survey ends; if they respond "yes," the survey branches to 20 items inquiring about what they consumed. Participants will discern that one survey path is much quicker, and some of them will respond "no" occasionally just to save time and trouble. One would think that participants would ignore the survey instead of taking the short branch, but incentives for high response rates—such as entry into a raffle for people who complete at least 70% of the surveys (see Chapter 5)—can perversely encourage deceptive and inattentive responses over nonresponse.

A good solution is to equate the length of survey branches. In our eating example, all surveys have 5 items, the "yes" branch adds 15 items, and the "no" branch adds zero items. Researchers can add items to the "no" branch, perhaps 10 to 15, that make it roughly as long. These padding items are usually bland, filler questions, but with some thought and creativity you might see the empty branch as an opportunity to measure interesting constructs that enrich your project or provide pilot data for a secondary hypothesis.

As a final tip, avoid too many layers of conditional branching. Your data file will get sparse when the main survey branches to increasingly skinny limbs. If some participants never reach a skinny limb—they never responded "yes," "yes," "no," for instance, to three layers of branching—then their data will be fully missing for that last layer. Unless the last data layer represents a common situation, analyses of the responses will involve a large cluster of participants with 100% missing values, a cluster of participants with only a few responses, and a cluster of people who have enough responses to analyze credibly.

Randomizing

Unless you're using paper diaries, in which case we applaud your old-school ways, your survey method has options for *randomizing* the order of your items. Shuffling your items has many virtues. After completing the same 10 items about their emotions a dozen times, participants can tacitly predict the items (e.g., that "happy" will follow "bored") and might start responding based on habit or autopilot rather than on how they are feeling at the moment. Randomizing the items prevents participants from forming habitual response patterns, so it's a useful way to encourage variable and valid responses.

The simplest kind of randomization is to randomize all the items. If your survey has 10 items, for example, you can present all 10 items in a different random order each time. In practice, however, randomization is usually constrained. Items usually sort into blocks, such as a cluster of six items about emotions and four items about current activities. Researchers could randomize the items within the blocks (i.e., the six emotion items appear in a random order) as well as randomize the blocks themselves (i.e., sometimes the six emotion items come before the four activity items).

You'll rarely want to randomize every item. As we discussed earlier, surveys should ask items about focal constructs first, especially fleeting experiences that benefit from interruption. Constructs that are less important and less fleeting can go at the end. But you should consider randomizing within blocks and between blocks when it makes sense for your project.

MEASUREMENT REACTIVITY

Measurement reactivity—the simple fact that the process of measurement can shift the measured scores—is one of the most interesting and vexing aspects of behavioral research (Webb et al., 1966). Daily life studies have all the usual reactivity features that are inherent in self-report surveys, such as factors that cause people to give misleading, desirable responses (e.g., because they are feeling watched or judged) or careless, inattentive responses (e.g., completing an overly long or confusing survey). Repeated assessment, however, is a unique aspect of reactivity that irks daily life researchers. Unlike cross-sectional studies, daily life studies will ask the same questions dozens of times. The dense, intensive assessment designs in daily life research naturally raise questions about whether the assessment process is shaping people's responses.

In our experience, the "reactivity question" is the most common one you will get from reviewers, thesis committees, and audience members (see Chapter 8). And it's a sensible question. Paying attention to one's behavior and tracking it via diaries—whether the behavior is money spent, cigarettes smoked, hours slept, words written, or apple fritters gobbled—

is a time-honored tool for enhancing motivation and changing behavior (Korotitsch & Nelson-Gray, 1999). You needn't be a crotchety skeptic of daily life research to wonder if asking depressed adults to reflect on and describe their emotions, symptoms, and self-esteem twice daily for 5 months might somehow change their responses (Vachon et al., 2016).

The large methodological literature on reactivity in daily life studies doesn't offer a simple answer to the reactivity question. Overall, the literature shows that reactivity tends to be small or minimal (e.g., De Vuyst et al., 2019; Stone et al., 2003), so it is usually a much smaller issue than people would think. On the other hand, some studies do find reactive effects of repeated assessment. It commonly looks like temporal shifts in people's responses over the course of the study, such as a decline in how often people smoke in a diary study of cravings and smoking cessation. Reactivity can be subtle, however, such as reduced variability in people's responses (Vachon et al., 2016), large shifts early in the study as people adapt to the items and procedure (Shrout et al., 2018), or interactions with person-level factors (e.g., repeatedly asking about happiness has different effects depending on prestudy happiness levels; Conner & Reid, 2012).

We favor Barta et al.'s (2012) perspective on reactivity. They view reactivity as a feature of a study, not of a method. "Is daily life assessment reactive?" is thus an inane question akin to "Do self-report scales have good internal consistency?" Sometimes it is, so instead of waving away the awkward issue of reactivity with some citations to past studies that didn't find it, researchers should seek to understand when reactivity is more or less likely. This knowledge can empirically inform study design and interpretation.

Barta et al. (2012) distilled the literature into a handful of factors that should attenuate or amplify reactivity. Exhibit 3.3 describes these factors, which come from the large research literature on how monitoring and tracking one's behavior leads to behavior change (Korotitsch & Nelson-Gray, 1999). Barta et al.'s framework helps explain why reactivity tends to be low but is occasionally high. In most experience sampling studies in personality psychology, for example, people are asked about a large set of experiences that are relatively mundane (e.g., moods and social encounters), with little motivation or pressure to change. The usual assessment methods conceal their past responses, so people can't use those as feedback. In contrast, some studies of smoking and problem drinking will have participants who feel motivated or pressured to change their behavior, which is often the focal behavior that is assessed. Continually monitoring this focal behavior can raise their awareness of its frequency and create opportunities for feedback, especially if they record their smoking or drinking on paper diaries.

EXHIBIT 3.3. When Are Daily Life Surveys More Reactive?

1. **When prestudy awareness and reflection are low.** For some behaviors and experiences, people lack awareness of or insight into when and how often they happen. Before participating in a study, people may not have thought about how many times a day they check their phone, smoke a cigarette, hug or kiss their spouse, go to the bathroom, complain to a coworker, or hear music in their mind that isn't playing in the environment. In contrast, people are usually tuned into their emotional states and feelings of pain, energy, and fatigue. Reactivity is more likely when people are asked to repeatedly track and describe something they haven't thought much about before.

2. **When people feel motivated or pressured to change.** Monitoring a behavior, not surprisingly, provokes more reactivity when people are motivated to change it. In research studies, participants can be motivated to change for inner reasons, such as in studies of nicotine use, academic success, or marital conflict. Tracking and describing cigarettes smoked, hours studied, and conflicts averted will probably lead to shifts in how often these behaviors happen over the course of the study. In other cases, participants feel external demands to change their responses, such as the social desirability of the topic (e.g., studies on risky sexual practices, problem drinking, or intimate partner violence).

3. **When people focus on a single behavior.** Reactivity is more likely when only one behavior is assessed. If a survey is solely about what people eat, whether they smoked, or if they fought with their partner, then completing the survey dozens of times is more likely to change the focal behavior. But if a survey is about many things, then no single topic becomes salient, and reactivity is less likely.

4. **When people describe their behavior beforehand.** Asking people about what they will do is more reactive than asking them what they have done. For example, asking participants in a nicotine use study if they expect to smoke within the next 30 minutes will be more reactive than asking them if they have smoked in the past 30 minutes.

5. **When people get feedback about responses and patterns.** As anyone who has learned that they walked 9,937 steps so far that day knows, popular life-hacking tools motivate people by giving them feedback on their actions. Concrete behavioral knowledge is oddly motivating and increases reactivity in research studies. Fortunately, in most modern daily life studies, participants have no access to their prior responses and get no feedback. This prevents them from discerning trends over time, such as whether they're exercising more or complaining less since the study started. When participants can see their prior responses (e.g., when paper diaries or notecards are used), people can use their early surveys as benchmarks for change.

In sum, there's no simple answer to give to someone who asks about whether your study was afflicted by reactivity. On the one hand, it's obvious from the body of methodological work that repeated assessment is not nearly as troublesome in daily life work as one might think. But on the other hand, researchers can be cavalier about waving off methodological problems when it's in their interest to do so, so we encourage readers to take a critical and humble perspective on their studies, using the factors in Exhibit 3.3 as a guide.

CONCLUSION

Coming up with a sampling framework and a set of items for your first project can be intimidating, but we encourage you to start with designs and items that have worked for established labs studying similar populations. With pilot testing and experience, you'll find it easier to strike a balance among days, beeps, and items and to craft items that make sense for your participants and their daily environments. Now that you have a design and a survey, how will you collect the data? In the next chapter, we show how to think through your many options for signaling participants and collecting survey data.

4 SELECTING A SYSTEM FOR SIGNALS AND SURVEYS

When daily life researchers get together, they usually gossip about their systems for data collection: what people are using to send beeps and collect data, how much they like it, and what shiny new options are on the horizon. By *system*, we mean the methods a research group uses for the two fundamental tasks: *signaling participants* and *collecting data*. New researchers, in our experience, want to jump straight into picking a research system, usually something high tech and fancy that they saw at a conference. But picking a system for daily life research is not something to take lightly. Once you choose one, you're committing to a significant up-front investment in research infrastructure: learning the system, training staff, developing manuals and materials, and buying software and equipment. Once you're set up, time and money are big barriers to switching.

Instead of reviewing specific systems currently in use, we think it is more valuable to step back and consider data collection more abstractly. How do your options vary? What general issues should you think about when deciding how to send signals and collect data? What do experienced researchers wish they had considered when they were new to daily life

https://doi.org/10.1037/0000236-004
Researching Daily Life: A Guide to Experience Sampling and Daily Diary Methods, by P. J. Silvia and K. N. Cotter
Copyright © 2021 by the American Psychological Association. All rights reserved.

EXHIBIT 4.1. 10 Things to Consider When Evaluating a Daily Life System

1. Does the system send signals, collect data, or both?
2. Is the equipment yours or theirs?
3. Can participants ignore or control the signal?
4. How does time get stamped?
5. Do missed surveys vanish?
6. How convenient is the survey process for participants?
7. What are the initial and ongoing costs?
8. Does it suit the participants and their environments?
9. How much training will personnel and participants need?
10. How private is data collection, and how secure are the data?

methods? Learning how to think about daily life systems will help you understand why there's no ideal system for every research design, participant population, and scientific question. You might even conclude that the low-tech classics are the wisest choice.

Here are 10 questions to consider when designing your study (see Exhibit 4.1). Devices come and go, as those of us with dozens of bricked Palm Pilots know, but these underlying research issues won't change.

1. DOES THE SYSTEM SEND SIGNALS, COLLECT DATA, OR BOTH?

The two basic requirements for self-report daily life research are (a) signaling participants and (b) collecting self-report data. Some systems do only one of these tasks; some do both. Your intuition might suggest that a system that does both is better, but there's no best way for all participant populations and research questions. When planning a daily life study, it is clarifying to see signaling and surveying as distinct methodological tasks.

Exhibit 4.2 lists common ways of signaling participants. For intensive, within-day sampling—such as an experience sampling study—you should use a device that people carry with them, such as a phone, tablet, or watch. This allows people to receive signals as they change locations throughout their day. For infrequent surveys—such as a daily diary study—you can use systems that people interact with more rarely, such as email accounts and physical mailboxes.

For collecting data, modern work has settled into a handful of methods. Exhibit 4.3 lists the most common tools for self-report data. Most of them are digital these days, from apps running on a portable device to web-based surveys accessible from computers and smartphones. But the older classics, such as interactive-voice-response (IVR) telephone systems and paper diaries,

EXHIBIT 4.2. Some Common Ways to Signal Participants

- **Participants' own brains.** In event-based sampling designs (see Chapter 2), participants must themselves detect that a survey-triggering event has happened and remember to complete a survey.
- **SMS text messages.** Participants receive a text message on their phone that tells them it is survey time. The message usually includes a link that participants can tap to go directly to a web survey.
- **Beeps, rings, and buzzes.** Participants hear a beep, ringtone, or vibration from a pager, Palm Pilot, digital watch, cell phone, smartphone, smartwatch, or tablet that they carry with them. They might complete the survey on the same device that signaled them.
- **Email.** Participants receive an email message as a signal, usually with a link to a web-based survey. This method is common for designs with infrequent surveys, such as daily diary designs.
- **Phone calls.** Participants receive a call on their phone, usually sent from an automated interactive-voice-response (IVR) system, as a signal. This method works on all phones—the participants' own smartphones, cheap flip phones that the researcher bought and passed out, or landlines at the participants' residence.

remain popular and widely used. As we'll see when discussing the other nine questions, each approach has some advantages for different problems and populations.

2. IS THE EQUIPMENT YOURS OR THEIRS?

Do the devices used for signals and surveys belong to you or to the participants? In the past, daily life research usually required the researchers to buy a fleet of devices—beepers, programmable watches, and Palm Pilots—to loan to participants. With the advent of home computers and cell phones, daily life researchers started taking advantage of what their participants already owned. And now that cell phones and smartphones are ubiquitous, researchers commonly rely on participants' own possessions for signals and surveys (Harari et al., 2016; Miller, 2012). Ironically, the most low-tech method—paper diaries—is the one that relies on researchers the most: It would be rude to expect participants to make their own photocopies of the surveys.

When selecting a system, researchers must discern what they can realistically expect their participants to own. Be thoughtful, inclusive, and informed—it's easy to slip into egocentric assumptions and lazy stereotypes. For many populations, you can expect the participants to have home access

EXHIBIT 4.3. Some Common Ways of Collecting Surveys From Participants

- **Paper surveys.** Participants receive paper surveys from the researchers and complete them when signaled. They either get all the surveys up front (e.g., a pile of 30 surveys at the start of a 30-day diary study) or in batches (e.g., batches of seven are distributed weekly). To retrieve the completed surveys, researchers include self-addressed, stamped envelopes; ask participants to drop them off at the research lab periodically; place a secure dropbox in a convenient location (e.g., for research in a workplace or school setting); or collect them in person.

- **Web surveys.** Participants complete the survey online on a web-based survey platform. Participants access the survey via a web link, and the data accumulate in the cloud and can be accessed only by research staff with the required log-in credentials. Because many colleges and universities already have an institutional site license for a secure survey platform, web surveys are popular, inexpensive, and well worth a look from researchers who wish to dip their toes into daily life methods.

- **Phones.** Using an interactive-voice-response (IVR) system, participants can complete a survey on any telephone, from old-school landlines to modern smartphones. Researchers record the survey items by speaking them aloud, and participants hear the items through the phone's speaker. To respond, participants press digits on the phone's keypad for numerical responses (e.g., pressing 2 to rate an item on a 5-point Likert scale) and speak into the phone for open-ended items. The data reside on a computer or server controlled by the researchers; no data are stored on the phone. IVR systems can call participants for random-interval designs, or participants can call into an IVR system for event-based and daily diary designs. Although phone calls seem quaint, IVR methods have superior privacy and security features.

- **SMS text messages.** Survey items can be given via texts, much like an IVR phone system. People receive a survey item via text (e.g., "Right now, how HAPPY are you?") and respond by texting back a response (e.g., the number 4 for a 1-5 Likert item) or via typing for open-ended items.

- **Palm Pilots.** Palm Pilots were the original "killer app" for experience sampling (Le et al., 2006). Researchers could load a program onto the device that would send signals and ask questions; participants answered by tapping the black-and-white LCD screen with a stylus. The data resided on the device and had to be downloaded manually. Although largely obsolete, Palm Pilots still provide trusty service to a few throwback research groups.

- **Apps.** Sophisticated survey apps can be installed on tablets, smartphones, and similar portable devices (e.g., iPods); smartwatches are an intriguing emerging technology for app-based assessment (Intille et al., 2016). App systems typically afford complex signaling for experience sampling studies as well as participant-initiated surveys for daily diary and event-based studies. Most app-based systems upload the data directly to a secure online portal via the device's WiFi or data network functions.

to a phone and the internet. For many others, you can expect access to a cell phone or to a smartphone. But your population is much more diverse in its tech savviness, affluence, and economic stability than you think. Even in a sample of university students, not everyone has a stable residence to call home or enough food to last the week, let alone the latest four-figure smartphone. If we had a Palm Pilot for every time we heard a researcher say "Everyone has a smartphone these days!", we'd have a lot of dusty Palm Pilots.

The most obvious reason why researchers use their own devices is because participants tend not to own them, but there are other reasons. First, you can ensure consistency. Participants have different kinds of computers and phones, from big and shiny to cracked and crusty, and they use different programs for emailing, texting, typing, and web browsing. This variability doesn't matter for most projects, and it is usually a virtue. Many people with disabilities, for example, have assistive software installed on their phones and devices, from screen readers that speak your survey aloud to apps that coerce a color-blind–friendly palette. But if a consistent user experience is important, distributing devices to all participants ensures a standard experience. Second, for some projects, distributing your own devices can address complex data security and privacy issues and give you more control over what the device can and can't do. Finally, using your device can sometimes be a perk of participating, such as when participants who are unemployed or homeless can use a cell phone for personal use throughout an IVR study.

If you distribute devices to participants, you should plan for the big three: damage, loss, and theft. These apply both to the device and to accessories like chargers, cases, batteries, adapters, cables, and styluses, which are more likely to vanish than the device itself. For damage, even careful participants will occasionally drop a device, bang it against a table or doorway, or spill drinks on it. Many a Palm Pilot has fallen to a watery grave in a toilet. Your fleet of devices should be larger than necessary so you can replace damaged ones, and you'll need a plan for getting replacement devices to participants midstudy.

Device loss is much less common than damage, in our experience, and theft is extremely rare. Nevertheless, prevention is the cure for most cases of loss and theft. Marking the devices—via engraving, permanent labels, and university asset barcodes—both discourages theft and provides contact details for whoever finds a wayward device. You can reduce theft by avoiding devices that are cool and alluring. Any small digital device with high resale value invites temptation, so consider functional and frumpy ones instead. In our experience, participants take unusually good care of our devices, but part of the research procedure is discussing the importance of caring for the device and what to do if it malfunctions (see Chapter 5).

The obvious benefit of relying on participants' own devices is that it is cheaper and simpler in many ways: buying, maintaining, and securing a big fleet of electronic devices is expensive. But the biggest advantage, especially for studies that use intensive within-day sampling, is that participants are motivated to carry their own device around with them as they go about their daily lives (Burgin et al., 2012). Instead of trying to remember to take a tablet with them to work, participants can simply take their own phone with them like they always do. As a result, we will get a more accurate view of the day when people respond to signals wherever they are.

A related benefit is that compliance rates—the percentage of surveys that participants complete—should go up when people use a device that they're motivated to keep close at hand. In the old days of Palm Pilot studies, for example, we commonly saw "missing days" in which none of the surveys were completed. Participants often said that they forgot the Palm Pilot at home or forgot to charge it. This was surely true sometimes, but it was obvious that people would deliberately leave the Palm Pilot at home on days when they didn't want to lug it around and hear its shrill, howling signal. By contrast, participants are rarely without their personal phones in the modern era of smartphone addiction, so compliance rates should be better. A study that compared smartphones with paper diaries, for example, found that participants often forgot to carry the paper diaries but rarely forgot their smartphone (Laughland & Kvavilashvili, 2018).

In practice, many research projects are a mix of your devices and theirs. When collecting data with smartphone apps, for example, you'll encounter participants who don't have smartphones and a few others whose phones lack the operating system or storage space to run the app. Many participants still don't own a cell phone or don't have stable access to one, so the researchers would need a small fleet of loaner phones for an IVR study. And some participants simply prefer not to use their own device, usually because they are wary about data privacy or resource limits (e.g., using up minutes, texts, or data for the study), so you'll need some loaner smartphones or tablets. Finally, it's wise to plan for a "better than nothing" backup—often an emailed link to an internet survey or a batch of paper diaries—in case a participant has an unexpected tech calamity.

3. CAN PARTICIPANTS IGNORE OR CONTROL THE SIGNAL?

Can participants ignore or mute the signal you send them? For most modern methods, participants can control the intrusiveness of the signaling. If the signal involves sending emails, participants can avoid checking their email.

If the signal involves texting, calling the phone, pushing an app notification, or triggering an alarm, participants can usually mute it by turning down the device's volume, putting it in a "do not disturb" mode, or powering it down.

Some apps and devices, however, can create obligatory signals that participants can't mute or prevent. The old-time Palm Pilots, for example, were notorious for their loud, clanging klaxon that could be silenced only by starting a survey. Some modern apps can hijack the device so that it wakes up and makes noise even if a participant has muted the device or put it in sleep mode.

Researchers should decide if they want an ignorable or an obligatory signal. One size does not fit all, and we recognize there are samples and research questions where imposing a loud signal is the best choice. In general, though, we agree with the view that researchers should "design assessment equipment with 'livability functions'" (Black et al., 2012, p. 342). Most daily life researchers believe that data quality is higher when participants can integrate the device into their daily habits, which sometimes involves ignoring signals. Participants are usually good-natured and willing to put up with some inconvenience for the sake of science, but your study is not so important to them that they'll harm their well-being and relationships. When participants can't mute a loud device, they are more likely to leave it muffled in a sock drawer all day than run the risk of it interrupting a crucial meeting with their boss, blaring during class on test day, disrupting family dinner, or waking up the baby. Livability aside, you should consider sample-specific safety issues before imposing uncontrollable signals, such as whether participants might be driving, operating equipment, or undertaking activities where their safety would require preventing loud, unexpected interruptions.

4. HOW DOES TIME GET STAMPED?

How does your system record time? Ideally, it should accurately stamp times for both signals and surveys. For signals, it helps to know when a signal went out, such as when the phone rang, the app notification popped up, or the automated email reminder to do an end-of-day survey later was sent. Time stamps for signals are usually used for troubleshooting and quality control—ensuring that the signals arrived and at the right times—rather than for substantive research questions.

For surveys, on the other hand, accurate time stamping is crucial. Survey time plays two roles. First, time is an interesting psychological variable in many daily life studies. Time points (e.g., whether something happened in the morning or evening) and time intervals (e.g., the temporal distance between events) are interesting in their own right and necessary for estimating within-day trends (see Chapter 7). Second, time stamping is required for screening data and flagging aberrant survey responses, a topic we examine in detail in Chapter 6. Ideally, a system should provide accurate time stamps for when participants started a survey and when they finished it. This allows you to check if people started the survey at the right time (e.g., within 5 minutes of a signal) and if they completed it within a normal time span (e.g., a 15-item survey should take no more than a few minutes). Some systems afford finer levels of time stamping, such as when participants initiated and responded to each survey item, but overall start and end times are enough for most purposes.

The worst way to stamp time is to ask participants to do it. Because early diary research relied on paper diaries, the validity of self-reported time stamps preoccupied early methodological studies (e.g., Green et al., 2006; Lane et al., 2006), and a large literature now shows that self-reported time is unreliable. Several studies have asked people to record when they completed a survey while surreptitiously recording the time, such as with sensors attached to the binder that contained blank surveys. It turns out that participants commonly lie about the day and time of dairy completion, usually because they are cranking out several days of diaries at a time (e.g., Stone et al., 2002).

Passive time-stamping methods that don't require participant input are thus best. As a caveat, however, digital clocks are flakier than people think and can significantly drift across days and weeks (see Exhibit 4.4). Unless a device calibrates to a master clock—via radio signals, cell towers, or online servers—its accuracy will slowly erode, especially if it is battery powered and exposed to temperature changes (e.g., F. L. Walls & Gagnepain, 1992). The clocks for devices that aren't connected to the internet should be inspected regularly to ensure their accuracy.

A final quirk of time-stamping concerns ecological changes in time—when the time in the participants' environment shifts. The most common one involves time zones. Some of your participants might not be in your time zone, and others might travel across time zones over the course of your project. You should understand how your system handles time zones before collecting data. Many digital systems handle this well, either by expressing all times in the participants' local time or in a universal time zone. Ideally, the system will detect the time zone instead of asking participants which zone they are in because a startling number of grown adults will give the wrong time zone (e.g., around 35% in one recent study; Harper et al., 2020).

EXHIBIT 4.4. Segal's Law and Those Digital Clocks

If it seems like we're belaboring the flaws of digital clocks, consider Segal's Law, the old adage that states, "A person with a watch knows what time it is; a person with two watches is never sure." When a project uses two devices, each with its own clock, time stamps become complicated when one or more devices slips out of alignment. Time slippage is less common with self-report methods, which tend to use systems with reliable time coding. But for research that uses other portable devices to measure behavioral, physiological, and environmental stimuli, the alignment of time can get tricky.

One kind of error is random. The inner clock on a wrist actigraph or ambulatory physiological monitor, for example, will slowly slip out of alignment relative to the device that sends signals or collects surveys. This random error is irksome but small compared with systematic error, which usually comes from time zones and daylight savings time. The inner clocks on "dumb" devices don't adjust for time zones and rarely adjust for daylight savings time. As a result, the time stamped by your device that adjusts (e.g., a smartphone app) can be off by an hour or more from the time stamped by the device that doesn't. Even worse, this systematic bias will vary by participant (e.g., some will change time zones and others won't) and by time of year (e.g., the data collected before daylight savings time may be accurate but the data collected afterward may be off by 60 minutes).

A related vexing issue concerns seasonal clock changes, such as daylight savings time. Most digital systems will automatically adapt to new times, but some won't. If the devices are in service during a seasonal clock change, you'll need to keep tight records and correct the time stamps when cleaning and prepping the data (see Chapter 6).

5. DO MISSED SURVEYS VANISH?

What happens when participants miss a survey? Can they access the missed survey later on, or does it vanish? In daily life research, we would prefer for participants to miss a survey than to complete it days later: "missing data over misleading data" is our motto. Daily life methods are motivated by the goal of measuring events and experiences as close to when they happen and where they happen, within the project's constraints. Allowing participants to fill out a survey long after the signaled time defeats the point of daily life assessment.

Your signaling and survey system should have a way of handling missed surveys. The first and best way is to make missed surveys vanish, thus preventing participants from accessing and completing them at a later time. Because this issue is close to the hearts of experience samplers, most methods used in intensive sampling (e.g., smartphone apps and IVR text and phone systems) have functions to close and conceal missed surveys within a window specified by the researchers, such as 5, 10, or 30 minutes. For web surveys, researchers should examine their platform's options for opening and closing surveys. For example, if participants receive a daily email with a link to that day's survey, can they dig into their old messages and access the surveys from the missed days? A second way is to flag surveys completed at the wrong time. When your time stamps are accurate, you can screen out responses that were submitted at aberrant times (see Chapter 6).

The availability of missed surveys bedevils projects using paper diaries. In a daily diary design that lasts 30 days, for example, simply giving people 30 surveys and collecting them a month later enables participants to complete them in batches. Plenty of studies have found poor compliance for paper surveys (Tennen et al., 2006). Participants will complete them in batches to please the researchers and to qualify for incentives, such as entry into a raffle if 75% of the surveys are completed. Unless a paper survey is collected daily, completed or blank, participants can always go back and fill out a missed day.

6. HOW CONVENIENT IS THE SURVEY PROCESS FOR PARTICIPANTS?

Participants ignore signals, so missing data plagues daily life research (see Chapter 6). Prevention is the best cure for participant nonresponse, so a survey system should be intuitive and convenient for the participants. By reducing the hassle and friction of providing data, we can nudge participants to provide more of it. Pilot testing your survey with yourself, your research assistants, and a few pilot participants will give you a good sense of the sources of friction in your survey and any opportunities to trim items.

Intuitiveness and convenience depend on the population you are studying, but a good metric for comparing survey options is *survey time*—how long it takes to complete a survey. The same set of self-report items will take much longer on some devices than others. One study, for example, randomly assigned participants to do a week of experience sampling using a Palm Pilot or an IVR system with their own cell phone (Burgin et al., 2012). With Palm Pilots, participants read the item and respond by tapping the screen, just like on modern app-based systems. With IVR systems, participants lift the phone to their ear, hear the item read aloud, and then bring the phone down to so they can see and use the touchpad—a longer, more awkward process. The same survey took just under a minute (55 seconds) on the

Palm Pilot but much longer—around 2.5 minutes (159 seconds)—on the IVR system. Shorter survey times should foster higher response rates, and participants did indeed have better compliance rates with the Palm Pilots (70%) than the IVR system (51%).

Aside from length, some surveys are more convenient for people to complete in the hurly-burly of daily life. An intriguing example comes from a study of smartwatches (Intille et al., 2016). The researchers compared a common, phone-based approach (a six-item survey given six times per day) with a smartwatch that interrupted people almost constantly—roughly every 25 minutes—but asked only a single question each time. This "micro-EMA" approach interrupts people much more often, but the study found that participants in the smartwatch condition rated the study as much less distracting and completed the surveys at much higher rates (81% vs. 65%).

7. WHAT ARE THE INITIAL AND ONGOING COSTS?

Unless you are made of money, you should consider how much all of this will cost. You can do only what you can afford, and many researchers cobble together inexpensive systems from existing resources. You can do some righteous daily diary studies, for example, with an email account and access to a web-based survey platform that your university already pays for. Photocopied paper diaries are bad for trees but good for your research budget.

Researchers often buy software licenses and devices during the boom times, such as when they get a grant or receive start-up funds at a new job. If you expect to do daily life research for more than 5 years, you should consider whether your system is sustainable when the grant ends, the start-up funds are gone, the research assistants are fewer, and the university is in its usual budget malaise. Could you still afford to pay for annual access to the app-based system, for the IVR system's many phone lines, for the private server's upkeep, or for the SMS system's texting charges? Can you afford to repair and replace your aging, broken, and missing devices? Researchers often don't realize the enormous investment they have made in learning the system, training the team to use it, developing manuals and documentation, and securing research ethics approval, so they can get stuck with a system that is increasingly unaffordable.

The future is a hazy place, so you should consider the possibility that your system could become obsolete or unavailable faster than you think. It is easy, with hindsight, to see how pagers and Palm Pilots became obsolete, but at the time they were the coolest thing in daily life research. It seems like everyone has a smartphone and always will, but it isn't so certain that any particular operating system will be around 5 to 10 years from now. And you shouldn't bet on ongoing compatibility between a fleet of devices (e.g., tablets or smartphones) and an app-based system. As many researchers have learned the hard way, as app-based systems evolve, they require increasingly newer operating system levels, so the fleet of tablets you bought at the start of the project might not work by the project's end. Finally, you should consider what would happen if the hip tech company that makes your fancy app-based system simply went out of business, as so many have, or if the free, open-source system dies a slow death from developer neglect.

8. DOES IT SUIT THE PARTICIPANTS AND THEIR ENVIRONMENTS?

How well does your system "fit" your participants and their daily environments? If your population usually carries around a smartphone, checks email, and fills in web-based forms, most of the common systems will dovetail with your participants' everyday lives and habits. But daily life research is conducted with a wide array of populations, and some systems are poorly suited for some of them. It's easy to design a study for your population's modal member, but such a study will inevitably exclude much of the population. For more inclusive sampling, you'll need an informed view of not only your typical participants but also your possible participants.

One major issue is accessibility. Many samples will have high proportions of people with atypical vision and hearing, often from age-related changes. Some devices and systems are versatile. Online web surveys, for example, can be customized to suit participants who have a vision impairment or are color blind, and they run on browsers that are designed to mesh with screen readers and assistive software. Smartphone apps for experience sampling, in contrast, vary in how easily participants can customize basic features like color and text size. Another cluster of issues concerns language, literacy, and reading level. Many participants, for a variety of reasons, would rather hear the items spoken aloud, like an IVR system does, than read written text.

In some cases, the system doesn't fit the environments. Smartphones and tablets, for example, with their big fragile screens, are poor choices for data collection in rough-and-tumble environments or whenever you suspect the devices might be stolen or neglected. IVR systems remain popular for research with many populations because, aside from their excellent data security features, IVR systems can be run on cheap, rugged flip phones that can handle abuse and be easily replaced.

9. HOW MUCH TRAINING WILL PERSONNEL AND PARTICIPANTS NEED?

How hard will it be to teach people to use your system? Each method has two training costs. First, you will need to train participants how to use the system. Your data quality will suffer if your participants don't know how to interact with your signaling and survey system. Most modern systems are easy for participants to learn—they're probably used to clicking links in email, filling out surveys on computers or touchscreen devices, and messing around with a phone—and training participants is easier when they are using their own devices. When you loan devices to participants or install an app on their own device, you'll need more thorough training. For many populations, lower tech methods—IVR systems for landlines and cell phones, paper diaries, and daily web surveys—will be easier to teach and safer choices.

Second, you will need to train the research staff to operate the system. New researchers tend to underestimate the complexity and hassle of creating and maintaining the expertise needed to start and manage a new system. A system that is frictionless for participants is often complicated for research staff. Getting automated texts with links to web surveys is easy for a participant; learning to operate two different programs—one for registering phone numbers, creating randomized text schedules, and sending links, and another for capturing survey data—is more complicated. High-tech systems need ongoing monitoring and some expertise to troubleshoot when participants fail to get the calls, texts, emails, and app notifications that they ought to get. When selecting a system, then, think about how many research assistants you will need to execute a project, how long it will take to train them to a high standard, and how often the research staff will turn over during the project.

10. HOW PRIVATE IS DATA COLLECTION, AND HOW SECURE ARE THE DATA?

Collecting data in people's diverse natural environments raises complicated research ethics issues, particularly around privacy and data security. Your institutional review board (IRB) will be keenly interested in these aspects of your project, and woe will befall a researcher who buys an expensive experience-sampling system that the IRB later rejects as unacceptable. For daily life research, four privacy and security issues loom large.

First, how private is data collection as it happens? For most self-report methods, people are tapping on a phone, tablet, or keyboard. Given how much time people spend staring at a phone and tapping it these days, the process of data collection is reasonably private. Other people may be around, but the person's participation in a research project isn't obvious, and participants can take reasonable precautions to keep others from furtively viewing their responses. It's another story for non–self-report methods, such as clipping microphones that record random snippets of the day (Mehl & Robbins, 2012) or sense ambient noise (Washnik et al., 2016) to the participant's clothing; small, shirt-clipped cameras that take snapshots of the participant's environment at regular intervals (Brown et al., 2017); or physiological monitors that have conspicuous wires and electrodes (Cybulski, 2011; Kamarck et al., 1998) that prompt all the participant's friends to ask if something is wrong with their heart. These methods are outside of this book's scope, but researchers using them for the first time should consult with other researchers and their IRB before committing to equipment.

Second, how secure are acquired data? Unlike lab research, where the data are safely ensconced in the lab's file cabinet or server, daily life data often travel along with the participant. Because daily life research often asks sensitive questions about physical and mental health, close relationships, and risky or deviant behavior, researchers should fret about data security in the real world. Are the participant's data safe from curious roommates or jealous spouses? What would happen if the participant lost your device on a busy street? What might happen if the device were handled by a border official or police officer? Security issues are complex and evolving, but on the least insecure end we have batches of paper surveys. Even when completed surveys use a study ID instead of someone's name, anyone who can link the binder of surveys to the person—a roommate, nosy officemate, or police officer—will know who filled out all those items about binge drinking and risky sexual activity. On the highly secure end, we have IVR systems that use traditional telephony (not text messages) to collect data. No items or responses are stored on the phone—if someone grabbed the phone mid-survey, they would see only a series of key presses (e.g., 404#767143001)—and the data are secure against everything but a wiretap. In between we have a range of systems—online surveys completed on shared computers, smartphone apps that upload survey data on public WiFi networks—with a range of security and privacy issues.

Third, are the data secure from the participants themselves? Can participants hack into the system in a way that compromises their own data? For most modern methods, participants can't modify the survey itself, change how the system signals them, or access prior responses. For some classic methods, like venerable paper diaries, participants can often access prior surveys and change their responses. One would think that participants have better things to do than mess with your study, but about one in 500 of our Palm Pilot participants would inexplicably dig into the open-source software and modify it, such as changing the response labels from "Not at all" and "Very much" to "Hell no" and "Hell yeah."

And fourth, how secure are the data on the researcher's end? This involves the usual set of procedures for handling, storing, and sharing research data. Most modern methods aggregate the data centrally, such as a computer in the researcher's lab running IVR software or an online platform that gives surveys running in an online portal. Researchers will need to establish who has access to the raw data, especially if it is identified or potentially identifiable.

CONCLUSION

Daily life researchers are faced with the tyranny of choice. Technology has been a boon to daily life research, especially the proliferation of smartphones and the development of app-based methods. At the same time, one size definitely does not fit all when it comes to research tools, so in this chapter we have sought to teach new researchers how to think through their options so they can choose a method that fits their population, research question, and budget. Once you have a research system in place, be it a humble web survey or a shiny new app, the fun part starts—collecting data, the topic of our next chapter.

5 COLLECTING DATA

The drama of collecting daily life data has two acts: (a) planning, prepping, and piloting; and (b) collecting the data. It's natural to be impatient to get some data rolling in, but don't shirk the first step. A lot can go wrong in daily life research, so part of the craft of conducting high-quality daily life studies is nailing down the details and sanding down the rough edges before enrolling participants.

This chapter discusses the two acts of collecting data. First, we describe how to plan and pilot your daily life data collection procedures. Some of the things we pilot will be standard: Are there any typos? Do the questions appear in the correct order? Does the survey branch like it should? But there will also be other factors unique to daily life designs we need to double-check: Are signals arriving when they should? Do the questions appear properly on different types of devices? What happens when you restart the device or the battery dies? Second, we describe how to collect data, with a focus on keeping a hand on the wheel. How can we monitor ongoing data collection? What are good midstudy procedures for maintaining participant engagement? What factors predict response rates during data collection,

---

https://doi.org/10.1037/0000236-005
Researching Daily Life: A Guide to Experience Sampling and Daily Diary Methods, by P. J. Silvia and K. N. Cotter
Copyright © 2021 by the American Psychological Association. All rights reserved.

> **EXHIBIT 5.1. Steps for Preparing and Running a Daily Life Study**
>
> **Preparing Your Study**
>
> 1. **Piloting.** When piloting your study, identify how things should work (e.g., signal frequency, survey branching) and see if everything works as intended. Involving research assistants in this process is a great way to identify potential problems during the nuts and bolts of collecting data.
> 2. **Linking records.** Connecting all responses from each participant to one another is a vital, and sometimes vexing, piece of daily life research. Identify all the data collection platforms you're using to craft a foolproof, redundant method of linking a participant's scores.
> 3. **Training research staff.** Getting your research staff up to speed will take time. Having a manual with all the details and a streamlined script outlining the necessary components for initial sessions will provide a solid beginning for training new team members.
>
> **Running Your Study**
>
> 1. **Teaching participants about the study.** Because people will be taking part in your study outside the lab, participants need to understand what you're asking them to do and how to do it. Including a software or device demonstration and a practice survey during your initial session will help orient your participants.
> 2. **Tending the garden.** Once people have begun the daily life portion of the study, monitoring participant responding, looking for technical glitches, and checking in with participants will improve your data quality.

and what levers can we pull to boost compliance? Although each study will bring its own surprises, the advice in this chapter—summarized in Exhibit 5.1—will help your first project go well.

PREPARING TO RUN THE STUDY

Thorough pilot testing will prevent most of the problems that could afflict a study, so researchers should look carefully before they leap into the brambles of data collection. This section describes how to pretest the full lifecycle of your project, from scrutinizing the signals to training the research staff.

Nailing Down the Signals and Surveys

Before piloting your study, it's helpful to lay out what *should* be happening. First, when should participants be prompted to fill out surveys? If using a fixed-interval sampling design, lay out the times when surveys should be available for participants to complete and when the surveys time-out if left uncompleted. If using a random-interval sampling design, describe during what time frame surveys should be sent, how many surveys should be sent per day, and when the surveys should time-out if not completed. If you want participants to get reminders to complete surveys if they haven't been opened, when and how will the reminders be sent? For event-based surveys, will you remind participants that they should complete a survey when the event of interest occurs? If you're using any fancy signaling mechanisms (e.g., triggers based on people's location or ambient noise levels in their environment), what criteria should be met for a participant to be signaled? Just getting the surveys to participants can go sideways, so you should define the details of when, where, and how people *should* be receiving surveys.

Next, think about the survey itself. When we want to ask a few follow-up questions if someone gives a certain response, we will have different branches to our survey (see Chapter 3). For each survey, identify any branching and the questions people should answer for each branch—if someone answers "Yes," what items should they see next? Then consider the basic visual display of the questions. Do you expect each item to appear individually, or will there be multiple items per screen? Do you anticipate people needing to scroll to view items and, if so, how much scrolling is expected? Is it obvious that scrolling is needed, or could inattentive people miss the unseen items? Can people view or alter their responses before submitting the survey?

Third, how long should each survey take? When deciding on our signaling schedules, we have a general idea of the length of each survey (see Chapter 3), but only pilot testing can reveal the survey's typical duration. How long each survey takes has implications for both the amount of information we can gather and how many times we can ask people to take the survey. If it's shorter than expected, we can add a few more items or signals; if it's longer than expected, we should trim a few items or signals. Survey quirks are usually easy to fix, and identifying the likely places things could go wrong simplifies these corrections.

Finally, and perhaps most vexing, is understanding the ins and outs of any technology involved in your study. Most modern studies use some form of technology to signal people to complete surveys, to collect survey information, or both (see Chapter 4). The most common failure points are when your system restarts (e.g., a computer or server running an interactive-voice-response [IVR] system or texting service), the participant's device restarts, the device's battery dies, or internet service is lost. For each piece of technology involved in your study, how *should* the device or system deal with these situations?

For many of the app-based platforms, a dead battery or device restart won't be disastrous. These systems tend to run in the background even if the app is not open. But in some cases, participants may need to reopen the app or perform another action to continue receiving signals or submitting surveys. With other systems, such as IVR systems, find out what happens if power is lost. Do you have to manually restart the program? Are data lost? How long will it be until the system is operational again? For systems relying on internet access to send signals or submit surveys, what happens if there is no internet access, either for the researchers or the participants? In some systems, the signaling information is stored within the software and will continue to signal participants regardless of internet access; other systems may fail to send signals, or the device won't receive any sent signals if the device is not connected to the internet. Likewise, some systems will store a local copy of survey responses submitted with no internet access to upload to an online storage platform when internet access is restored; other systems may not register any submissions made without internet access. Understanding the behavior of the devices, software, and platforms will help you test your study under all these different conditions. Technology can simplify many things in daily life research, but it does introduce its own hurdles and headaches.

Piloting Daily Life Data Collection

Once you have nailed down how all the components of the study should be working, it's time to start piloting. Members of the research team involved in designing the daily life data collection should be involved in this process. Both the head honchos on the research team and the research assistants should take part in this early-stage testing. The senior members know how the study ought to operate, so they will notice subtle faults. The new research assistants, in contrast, will experience the study with fresh eyes and notice the quirks and rough edges that participants will experience. Take research assistants through the study as you would any participant and see if there are aspects of the instructions that provoke questions or confusion. Revise your instructions to participants if your research assistants have questions about specific parts of the procedure or if they point out any confusing material. Exhibit 5.2 contains some common questions participants have about daily life procedures.

During piloting, test all the possible ways people could take part in your study. If you are asking participants to use their personal phones or devices, what are the possible devices they can use? If you're using a

EXHIBIT 5.2. Common Participant Questions About Daily Life Research

Daily life studies are probably new to your participants, and unfamiliarity breeds questions. Below are some common questions people ask.

- **Signals and Surveys**
  - When will I get signals to do the surveys? How many days will I get them?
  - What happens if I miss a survey?
  - Can I start a survey and come back to it later?

- **Work, Class, and Other Conflicts**
  - I have [work/class/another conflict]. Will this be an issue?
  - Do you have a letter I can show my [boss/teacher] so they know about the study?
  - Can I mute the notifications when [I'm busy/I'm asleep/the baby is sleeping]?

- **Technical Issues**
  - I got a new phone/My phone broke. What should I do?
  - I can't open the surveys on my phone/computer. What should I do?
  - If I have questions or issues during the study, whom should I tell?

- **Compensation**
  - When will I get paid or receive my credits?
  - Will I not be paid or receive credits if I miss surveys?
  - How will I know if I did enough surveys to earn a bonus payment or raffle entry?

smartphone-based app, make sure all compatible operating system platforms are tested. Although the app developers may say the app will work essentially the same way on different operating systems, there will always be some differences. Push notifications, app setup, and survey completion may all look or work slightly differently. If participants will borrow lab-owned equipment, such as a tablet or smartwatch, make sure all devices in your fleet are operational and supported by the survey app. App software is consistently being upgraded and patched, and you might discover, as we have, that your devices' operating system version is woefully out of date and now incompatible with your survey app. If you are sending participants links to surveys, test how the survey works on a phone, tablet, and computer.

Once you've assembled your testing team and a variety of devices, it's time to see how all the pieces fit together. First, the testers should pay attention to the mechanics of the study. Distribute the outline you created about how everything *should* work and tell people to take note of deviations from what is expected. In some cases, this involves answering the surveys and checking that the questions branch properly; in other cases, you should purposefully ignore a survey to see if reminders function as expected and if surveys vanish as intended. There will probably be other quirks that pop up, such as operating system updates or getting a new phone, that may affect data collection and should be noted as well. Low-tech methods deserve as least as much usability testing. When using paper surveys, for example, how frequently do your testers forget to bring the surveys with them during the day, forget to complete them, or lose them altogether? Does your method for collecting surveys—in person, by mail, or with a secure dropbox—work as intended?

Second, people should examine the livability of the data collection process in their own daily worlds. If you're sending signals, do the survey times and intervals between surveys make sense? Researchers must balance the desire for a lot of data with the goodwill of their participants (see Chapter 3), and nothing beats acting as a pilot participant to illuminate whether you struck this balance. In theory, signaling people to complete a survey about every 30 minutes between 7:00 a.m. and midnight sounds fine, but when you're the one being pestered by constant notifications and reminders, you may feel the urge to "accidentally" turn on airplane mode or convert to digital minimalism. No one cares more about your project than you do, so if you feel mildly irked by completing the surveys, your participants will feel decidedly annoyed.

During your field test, do the items make sense when you're receiving them? Do they work in the context of your daily environment? Piloting serves as another opportunity to check if the item wording is apt for the different contexts of daily life. But also think about the repeated nature of the questions—are the surveys coming too close together, or too far apart? For example, asking people every 30 minutes if they have eaten a meal since the last survey is likely too frequent; asking once every 8 hours might be too infrequent. In a sample of college students, sending a daily survey about the nutritional contents of people's dinner at 5:00 p.m. is probably a bit early; in a different sample, it may be appropriate. Piloting will often inspire you to tinker with the timing and number of surveys.

Making Contingency Plans

After everyone has piloted the study for several days, it's time to make sense of what happened. Start with your outline about what should happen. Were there any things that went wrong for most people, or everyone? Did certain things go wrong for people using a certain type of device or operating system? Take note of what your testers noticed that didn't work. Next, did people encounter any unanticipated issues? Many issues are easy to fix; for others, you may need to contact technical support to ask how certain processes work (e.g., how app patches or version updates affect the performance of ongoing projects) or to report bugs.

Even if piloting went relatively smoothly and you need to make only a few minor adjustments, it's worth planning for a few worst-case scenarios. Electronic data collection systems—apps, websites, or IVR—have many virtues but also present many opportunities for things to go wrong. After you have a better sense of how your study looks for participants through piloting, consider the following scenarios:

- **What if someone's device isn't compatible with your system?** Although you have done your due diligence and tested your study on many different devices and device types, a participant's device may be quirky enough to not work with your system. Sometimes you'll be able to catch this during an onboarding session, but people may also encounter issues partway through data collection. What is your plan in these situations? If you have a fleet of lab-owned devices, you could arrange to loan one out for the remainder of their participation. Alternatively, having paper survey backups with a method of signaling participants to complete surveys (e.g., setting phone timers, texting a signal, providing an old-school pager) would do in a pinch. You'll also want to think about how to get the paper surveys to participants efficiently.

- **What if I run out of lab-owned devices to loan?** In situations in which participants can use their own devices or opt to use a lab-owned device, there is always a possibility of running out of lab devices to loan out. If you run out of devices and a new participant requests to use one, one possibility is to delay their participation until a lab device is returned by another participant; however, this may not always be an option. Once again, paper survey backups with an alternate signaling method could work.

- **What if my entire electronic system crashes?** This is the nightmare that plagues daily life researchers. In general, it is probably best to push the pause button on enrolling any new participants if you are having major issues with your data collection system, but you may have participants in the middle of data collection. Once again, paper backups can be an option, but depending on how far people are through the data collection period (e.g., 1 day out of 7 vs. 6 days out of 7), you may elect to terminate their data collection early.

These are a few scenarios you may run into when using electronic systems. What's most important is thinking through what you could implement at short notice to salvage data collection if disaster strikes.

Evaluating the Pilot's Data Files

The final step in piloting your study is verifying that the data are being recorded properly and intelligibly. If you're using paper surveys, this isn't hard. Enter a few surveys into your preferred statistical program or database (e.g., REDCap) and take note of any changes that could be made to the survey to make data entry more efficient, such as numbering each item. At this stage, it is also helpful to develop a codebook for manual data entry that includes which items correspond to which variable names, how each item is coded (e.g., Does a "Yes" correspond to a 1 or 0?), and any coding policies (e.g., methods for auditing and checking hand-entered data).

If you are using an electronic data collection method, you'll need to investigate the data more thoroughly. Expensive, high-tech systems can fail in spectacular ways. Exhibit 5.3 tells a few cautionary tales for readers who put too much faith in technology. Start by finding out how you extract data files from the platform and the formats that are available. Usually, data collection platforms make downloading data files relatively simple, but there may be some variation. In some systems, you might get a single file with all responses from all participants; in others, you might get a separate file for each participant or each response. Within a single system, you could specify how you want to extract the data, such as what information is included or what file type is used. Explore these options and determine which best suits your needs for screening, analyzing, and archiving the final data.

Once you have a file downloaded, figure out how the data are structured. Because daily life research involves repeated assessment of the same items, the data file will represent this in one of two forms: *wide* or *long* format. In wide format, each row represents a single participant and each response to a single item will be represented as a separate variable. For example, if one of your items is what time a participant woke up that morning, you will have a separate variable for each time a participant provides an answer. In long format, each row represents a single survey response, and participants will have multiple rows of data. In wide format, you'll end up with many variables and fewer rows; in long format you'll have a lot of rows with fewer variables (see Chapter 6 for more details). Next, see what information the data collection system automatically includes about responses. In addition to responses to the items, you may also be given the date and time of survey completion, a unique response identifier, how long survey completion took, records of when signals were sent, and what type of device was used. You may be able to customize which of these pieces of information is included in your data file, but it's good to understand everything that will be—or could be—included in your data file.

EXHIBIT 5.3. More Money, More Problems

You can do daily life research with methods grand and humble (Chapter 4), but the modern trend is for portable digital devices, such as app-based smartphone systems and wearable smart sensors. Consumer psychology tells us that people use price as a heuristic for quality (Dodds et al., 1991), and we suspect that researchers assume that an expensive system must be reliable. Modern systems have transformed daily life research, but you need to pilot test them within an inch of their life. In our long and painful experience, we have learned that any method that is expensive and labeled "smart" needs extra scrutiny. Here are a few true tales—many from our experience, a few from our close collaborators—about mishaps from expensive commercial systems and devices:

- When a survey app was updated to add many fancy-pants features that few people use, it could run only on newer Android versions. As a result, some researchers learned midproject that their fleet of older tablets was now bricked.

- A wearable sensor was designed to output a data file and a log file. Bizarrely, the data file and log file were time-stamped from different internal clocks. The data file's time automatically shifted in response to daylight savings time, but the log file's time did not. A device sampling hundreds of times a second thus had timing discrepancies of 60 minutes at certain times of the year.

- One pricey interactive-voice-response system became even more expensive when the researchers learned that the software would run only on an old version of Windows and with an ancient database program that was available only as a CD-ROM from eBay. Because the old Windows software was inherently insecure, the computer wasn't allowed to connect to the campus internet and thus couldn't be checked or managed remotely.

- One survey app signaled nicely and collected surveys with a sleek interface, and it was compatible with both Apple and Android devices. When the data files were inspected, however, no data were being written when the testers used Apple devices. The company scrambled to update their apps but couldn't work out the bugs.

- Another survey app, after a minor app update, would consistently write several duplicate rows of data for each survey submission—but only for Android devices.

- Many survey apps that run on Android devices, for whatever reason, work poorly with some device manufacturers' operating system. In our experience, the incompatible devices are either obscure models no one owns or the most ubiquitous models that all your participants own.

- One app-based system worked well in early testing, but after their first study the researchers couldn't download the data file from the online dashboard. It turns out the system had a hidden file size limit that high-volume experience sampling studies would blow through.

Finally, you'll want to do some basic quality checks on the data. What is most important to pay attention to during early piloting is the coding of responses to your items and correct handling of survey branching. Start with a visual inspection of the data. If you have survey branching, are responses missing where they should be missing? Do the values for each variable make sense given the item? Do they appear as text when you would rather have numbers, or vice versa? Next, run descriptive statistics and frequencies on the items: Are the ranges of possible responses correct? Do all response options show up properly? Are items recoded that should be recoded? In some cases, you can tell the data collection software to automatically recode values, but for other software you'll need to do this yourself. If your software doesn't have this feature, make a codebook and indicate which variables will need to be rescored and how this should happen. For example, different software could treat nominal categories differently. In some cases, the data file will list the text response; in others, the software will convert it to a numerical response. Once you're comfortable with the data structure, you've finished piloting.

Linking Records

A crucial component of preparing to conduct a daily life research project is determining how you will compile the final data set you will analyze. In standard lab-based research, this may involve downloading data files from several computers, merging the files, and cleaning the data. In survey work, it may be as simple as downloading a data file from an online dashboard. But in daily life research, this process gets complicated when you have several sources of data—such as cognitive tests, cross-sectional surveys, MRI scans, clinical interviews, and repeated daily diaries—collected on different systems. Before launching a daily life research project, you will need to make sure you can correctly match each person's complete set of scores across all sources of data (see Chapter 6).

To start, identify all your data sources and the ways in which the data will be collected. For the daily life portion of the study, will all responses be recorded on the same platform, or are multiple types of daily life data being collected? Do you have data spread across many dashboards, servers, local computers, and file folders? For example, in some studies (e.g., George et al., 2019; Lehman et al., 2015; Sperry et al., 2018) participants will complete self-report surveys and have physiological measurements (e.g., heart rate, respiration, sleep duration) taken through the data collection period. Both qualify as daily life assessments, but these will be collected using separate platforms. Are you collecting any data in your lab session?

Oftentimes, we are interested in how characteristics of a person (e.g., personality, brain network connectivity, performance on working memory tasks) relate to the data collected in daily life. We usually will ask people to complete different measures and tasks once before starting the daily life portion of the study. These surveys, tasks, or brain scans will typically be on a platform different from the one used for daily life data collection. Finally, we may also collect non–daily life data outside of the lab, such as an end-of-study survey or an in-person semistructured interview. These surveys may be on the same platform as the daily life or in-lab data collection, but they may also be collected using an additional platform.

Regardless of the number or type of data collection platforms used, you will need a foolproof—in the deepest, most literal sense of the word—system for linking people's responses across platforms and daily life submissions. Beginners, take note—we cannot exaggerate the importance of a foolproof system for linking records across platforms. One method for linking records is to assign each participant an ID you select. This ID would be entered into each data collection platform and used to correctly merge data files and connect people's responses. This could be input in a few different ways: Some software will automatically ask for an ID number for participants; in online survey platforms, asking for an ID number can be included as the first question; an ID can be written on paper data collection forms; or inputting the ID number can be included as a separate survey within your daily life data collection software. This option is straightforward but should be used only if trained members of the research team are the people entering the ID number. Asking participants to remember and enter a researcher-generated ID is decidedly not foolproof on its own, and it will result in incomplete linking for many of your participants.

If the research team is not able to input the IDs across all platforms for all participants, you will need to use a different method to link people's responses. Because participants should not be relied on to remember a specific code or ID to input themselves, another way to generate a unique identifier for each participant is to ask them the same series of questions on each platform. The questions you select should ask about things that won't change each time someone answers it—asking about someone's birth month or their mother's name will result in the same response each time you ask. Once you have chosen three or four questions, you can decide a way to generate a unique anonymous code for each participant. For example, if you ask people their birth month, their mother's first name, and their own first name, you can select the first three letters of the month, the first two letters of their mother's name, and the last two letters of their name as the code. Someone who was born in March, has a mother named Anna, and is named

Jack would have a code of *MarAnCk*. People won't have difficulty answering these questions consistently multiple times, and you will have a reliable way of linking records.

Regardless of which ID linking method you use, there may be one additional step in linking records depending on the way you are collecting daily life data. If you are using an app-based data collection method, most systems will automatically generate a unique code for a participant's device, account, or both. These app-generated codes will likely be a string of random letters and digits and not something you will want to use on all your platforms, but the app will record these unique codes in addition to people's responses for each submission. More details are given in Chapter 6 about preparing your data for analysis, but you should note that you may also need to use these app-generated codes in linking records in addition to the IDs you create.

No matter how carefully you craft your data-linking plans, there will inevitably be times when someone forgets to input the ID, inputs the incorrect ID, or makes a typo when entering their first name. To safeguard your data from human error, it's important to build in redundancy. For example, when using an app-based data collection system, create dummy accounts for participants using your ID number in the account registration. This protects the privacy of your participants, and if the ID is accidentally omitted within the app itself you still have the account registration with the ID information to link with your lab records. It also can be helpful to keep a paper record of linking information that is separate from other data. If you are using participant answers to questions to generate a linking code, ask participants these questions separately from other data collection in case someone makes a typo in one survey or you need to refer to it later.

You may also consider using a combination of your own IDs and creating IDs based on participant responses—if your IDs get mixed up, you can always check your linking based on participant responses. Because collecting daily life data is time consuming and intricate, losing any data is painful. Taking extra steps to minimize data loss is worth the effort.

Training Research Staff

Once you've worked through the kinks and quirks of your daily life data collection and study design, it's time to work on your procedure for training other members of the research team. This process will likely resemble what you already do to train research assistants, but there will be a few extra steps given the complexity of daily life studies.

You can start by compiling documentation that the full research team can use as references throughout the data collection process (Berenson, 2018). The major reference you will need to draft is a manual detailing all aspects of running the study, including aspects that research assistants are not responsible for. Although each study is unique, there are a few sections that should be included in any manual:

- **How are participants recruited and scheduled for sessions?** In some cases, participants will be recruited and scheduled though institutional research pool systems or online research panels; in others, participants will be recruited through flyers, emails, clinics, or recruitment tables and scheduled through contacting a member of the research team. Lay out all possible ways people can be recruited, how they will be scheduled for sessions, and where the research team can view scheduled sessions.

- **What preparation is necessary before each onboarding session?** This may involve emailing participants reminders about the sessions, setting up lab computers, entering IDs into lab devices that will be distributed to participants, and checking who is signed up for the session.

- **What needs to be done during onboarding, whether it is face to face in your lab or remote via the internet?** Daily life projects require teaching participants what to expect and training them to respond to and complete surveys. This will usually include instructions given to participants but may also involve setting up participant devices for daily life data collection or monitoring aberrant participant behavior during the session.

- **What needs to be done after participants embark on the daily life portion of the study?** You should try to monitor people's response rates during data collection, a task made much easier with high-tech methods. You might decide to email people during data collection to increase response rates or to tell people that they are finished with the study. If you're using paper surveys, you need a procedure for collecting and tracking surveys as they roll in. The most important thing is that your manual is detailed and includes all processes involved in running the study.

You should develop a script for study sessions and answers to questions participants frequently ask. In addition to any general descriptions about the study goals, your script should explain what participants should expect from the daily life portion of the study. In this explanation you should include how people will know when to complete a survey—will they be sent an app notification, receive a phone call for IVR responding, or catch and release a carrier pigeon with their daily diary each evening? People also need to be told how often they will be completing surveys, for how many days they will be answering surveys, and when and how they will be compensated for their participation.

Participants will ask a variety of questions (see Exhibit 5.2), so providing an FAQ sheet for research assistants can be helpful. Some of the questions will be consistent across different studies—Whom do I contact if I have issues? What happens if I miss a survey?—and others may be unique to that particular study, such as what certain terms mean. Participants will likely ask questions not on the FAQ sheet as well, but having this document prepared makes sure research assistants can answer the obvious ones. One way to refine these documents is to run the first few sessions yourself to see what in your explanation is not as clear as you would like, or which questions participants keep asking. You know the ins and outs of the study the best and can refine your manual, script, and FAQ sheet on the basis of these initial sessions so that things run smoothly once research assistants take over.

The research team will also need training with the technology involved with the study. If you're going low tech and using paper surveys, this is pretty simple—just make sure research assistants know how many surveys participants should be given and any other equipment (e.g., prestamped envelopes to return, instruction sheets) people need to take part. If there are technological aspects of your data collection, it's important for research assistants to have a basic understanding of how everything operates even if they won't be involved with all aspects of study administration. For an IVR study, this could involve showing research assistants how the system is programmed to contact participants, how the items are programmed into the system, or how the data are recorded by the system. In an app-based system, this may additionally include how to install the app on a device, how to enroll participants within the app, or how to input participant ID codes. In addition, you will want to discuss any quirks or common issues with the data collection system or specific devices—refer back to what you discovered when piloting the project. Your research assistants will likely be the ones interacting with participants and answering questions about any technology in the study, so it's important they understand these elements and can answer questions about them.

The final element of training the research staff is establishing the protocol for the study. You will have already developed the key document for this step—the study manual—during piloting and will need to walk your research assistants through the information. Although you will spend most of the time detailing what the research assistants will be responsible for, you should also explain all elements of the protocol so that research assistants can answer participant questions about the study. Just like with any other study, you will want to carefully walk through what the research assistants will be doing.

In addition to what research assistants will likely do for any study (e.g., getting participants settled in the lab room, explaining the study's purpose), daily life studies involve additional steps in preparing for sessions, such as checking the online data management system, registering participant devices, or entering participant IDs in multiple places. Go through these steps as many times as needed by having your research assistants running you or each other as a "participant." Once they have a handle on the steps of the protocol, it's time to start working with participants.

Given the complexity of daily life studies, it will be helpful to ease research assistants into running sessions independently. A first step can be having your research assistants shadow you during a session that you are running—they will see everything being set up for a real session, how participants act and what questions they ask, and how you interact with participants. Seeing the study in action will often prompt new questions from your research assistants, so regrouping and discussing the protocol again after everyone has observed a session will reinforce what they are learning. After the research assistants have observed you, swap roles and observe them. It's likely that on their first try research assistants will hit some bumps, so having you there will reveal their readiness. Eventually, your research assistants will have a handle on the protocol and will be comfortable running sessions by themselves. Once research assistants are at this stage, it's still a good idea to check in about issues they encounter during their sessions or questions that pop up over the course of data collection; these are good topics for your regular lab meetings.

RUNNING THE STUDY

A daily life project will run smoothly when the participants are informed and engaged. This section describes how to train your participants, monitor the stream of signals and surveys to prevent problems, and check in with them to promote engagement and compliance.

Teaching Participants About the Study

Daily life studies require a lot from participants, so we need to teach them what to expect and what to do during data collection. Typically, this training will take place during an initial in-person session. You should allot around 15 or 20 minutes to familiarize your participants with what they will be asked, how and when they will respond, and how to get in touch with the research team if there are questions or issues. Although most studies involve in-person meetings, fully remote data collection is increasingly popular and involves essentially identical principles for collecting quality data (see Exhibit 5.4).

The first step in training the participants is explaining the basics of what you will be assessing. In some studies, these constructs may be relatively concrete and easy for participants to understand, such as engaging in prayer

---

EXHIBIT 5.4. Fully Remote Data Collection

In this chapter, we describe how to launch a face-to-face daily life study. In the typical project, researchers and participants cross paths at least once (i.e., during the initial training) and often many times (e.g., midstudy check-ins, end-of-study meetings), especially if the daily life assessment is part of a bigger research project with other modes of data collection (e.g., clinical interviews, neuroimaging, and behavioral observations).

Nevertheless, many modern projects are fully remote—the researchers and participants never meet. The virtues of remote data collection are many:

- Many populations can't travel to your lab for reasons ranging from distance to disability.
- With remote methods, you can sample from established, well-characterized survey panels that are unavailable for in-person research.
- You can run a leaner lab with fewer research assistants.
- Remote methods afford huge samples of thousands of participants (e.g., Baumeister et al., 2019).
- Although it's a ludicrous possibility that would obviously never happen, your institution might shut down face-to-face research to stem the spread of a global viral pandemic.

We expect to see more fully remote data collection in the future, and we encourage researchers to consider remote methods when getting started. The process is simplified with app-based digital platforms, but you could run remote research by emailing links to web surveys or shipping people questionnaires with self-addressed postage-paid return envelopes. The materials might look different in remote projects, but the principles and best practices that apply to face-to-face projects—diligent pilot testing, good documentation, thorough research training, participant-friendly training materials, and ongoing survey monitoring and communication—are essentially the same.

(Olson et al., 2019) or sexting (Howard et al., 2019). In other cases, your research topic may be a bit fuzzier for participants, such as what counts as coworker incivility (Zhou et al., 2019), the specific Facebook engagement activities that qualify as "exploring" (Manuoğlu & Uysal, 2020), or anything that people don't often reflect on (e.g., musical imagery, mind-wandering; Cotter et al., 2019; Kane et al., 2017).

Before getting into the fine-grained details of your study, provide participants with a clear explanation of your research topic. This explanation should also include information about what "counts." If you're interested in smoking behaviors, what counts as having smoked? A single puff, or does the entire cigarette need to be smoked? If you're interested in disordered eating, which behaviors qualify? There may not be a single correct answer for what counts, but you and your participants need a shared understanding of your key variables. Defining your variables is especially important for event-based surveys because participants will need to know what behavior or state to monitor to know when they should answer a survey (Moskowitz & Sadikaj, 2012; Reis & Gable, 2000). You may find it useful to give participants a letter describing the concepts involved in the study or when they should complete a survey just in case they forget.

Depending on how you are collecting data, this information could be integrated into the data collection platform or in automated emails in which survey links are sent to participants. Finally, emphasize that people should complete the surveys only when it is safe and appropriate (e.g., don't do surveys when driving, operating machinery, or in social situations where it would be risky or inappropriate). These situations will be obvious to most participants, but we have found that our most diligent and perfectionistic participants need clear boundaries to discourage them from trying to complete every single survey.

After describing the topic of the research project, explain the parameters of the study to participants. The first set of parameters concerns the surveys. You will need to tell people how many surveys they will be sent each day, when the surveys will be sent during the day, for how many days they will be completing surveys, how long they have to complete each survey, and whether they can expect reminders if a survey isn't completed within a specified time frame. In some designs, you may not have exact answers for these. For example, if you are using random-interval signaling, you would not know the exact time someone will receive a survey, but you could say that people can expect surveys between noon and midnight and how many they should roughly receive. In a daily diary study, for example, people would be told to expect the survey every evening at exactly 7:00 p.m.

The second set of parameters concerns the study overall. The primary factor is what happens if someone misses surveys. In some cases, this isn't a big deal—in an experience-sampling study in which people are sent 60 surveys over the course of a week, missing five or six surveys likely won't be an issue. In a daily diary study, five or six missing surveys out of 14 can be problematic. For some event-based designs that aim for comprehensive event coverage, participants receive paper diaries as a backup for recording events that they missed on the digital device (e.g., Xu et al., 2018). Carrots and sticks for completing surveys should be thoroughly discussed. Many studies have escalating incentives or bonuses to motivate higher response rates; others use raffle entries for all participants who complete a certain number. Participants are keenly interested in the incentives and will have a lot of questions if the incentive system is tiered or complex.

The research assistants should walk through a practice survey with the participants. This allows the researcher to define terms, explain nuances of items, answer questions, and test how well participants understand the survey questions. Naturally, the practice survey should be completed in the same mode—paper diary, texted link, or app notification—as the real surveys. When creating the practice survey, make sure that people are exposed to all the items in the survey (i.e., eliminate any skipping, subsetting, or branching). You can explain that the survey is showing them all possible items and that the actual surveys will take less time, but people should be able to see and ask questions about everything they could be asked during the study. After people go through the practice survey, solicit questions and reiterate any important pieces of information people need about the surveys. This is the time to make sure everyone understands the survey items.

Even though you will thoroughly explain and walk people through the daily life portion of your study, it is inevitable that someone will forget part of the instructions, encounter a technology glitch, or want to know when they're finished with the study. Give participants a way to get in touch with you and the research team, such as a phone number or email address that is monitored during the data collection period. You may already have listed this type of information on your consent forms, but it's helpful to include it with the surveys as well. If you're using paper forms, add this to the bottom of the form; if you're using apps or emailed surveys, include contact information within the app or email. If participants will be using lab-owned equipment, include a business card in the device's case, or break out your label maker and stick your contact information right on the device. Few participants will contact you, but if something does go awry, they should know how to get in touch.

Tending the Garden During Data Collection

An ongoing daily life project needs constant tending. You will need to spend time monitoring participant engagement in the study, checking in with participants about tech issues, and contacting participants to encourage their continued compliance with the study.

Monitoring Survey Activity

Develop a way to monitor participant compliance during data collection to reduce missing data. Prevention is the cure for missing data (McKnight et al., 2007). Daily life researchers will never cure the malady of missingness, but that doesn't mean we should throw up our hands and say, "Whatever; the software can 'handle' missing data." Robust procedures for tracking and nudging participants as they move through the study will increase their engagement.

If you are using paper surveys, have people submit their surveys regularly, such as daily or weekly depending on the length of your study. When you receive their responses, you can track how many surveys people are completing, identify any participants who are nonresponsive or are not following study instructions, or confirm if people engaged in specific activities when instructed (e.g., if people are supposed to visit a clinician on Day 8 of a study and complete a survey about their experiences, did they do so?). Creating a spreadsheet or database to track compliance is important—identify what information you want to monitor and make sure to consistently monitor these features. At a minimum, you should track how consistently each participant provides responses.

If you are using a technology-based data collection method (e.g., app, IVR, or online survey platform), you'll have even more information available to track participant compliance. In many app-based data collection systems you can view when each participant last opened or refreshed the app, the start and end times of each submission, how many submissions people have provided, the time each survey was sent to participants, and whether people have deleted the app from their device. In online survey platforms you often can access information regarding when each survey was started and completed, meta-data about the type of device and browser used, or the location of survey submission. You will have already tinkered with what information your data collection system automatically collects when you piloted your study. In addition to monitoring response rates, you should regularly check when people last logged in to an app or when it last refreshed (if this information is available). Long periods of time without logging in or refreshing could indicate a technology issue that participants may not be aware of but that can be fixed.

Checking in During the Study

While monitoring their surveys, consider planning check-ins with your participants during data collection. These check-ins can be quite simple, such as sending an email to everyone partway through data collection just to ask how things are going, if people have experienced any problems, or if there are any questions. Oftentimes participants won't get in touch with you if there are problems or questions, but they may respond to an email if you ask about them. If there is something people need to do during a specific time window during data collection—return to the lab on Day 7 or visit a museum between Days 3 and 5—monitoring when each person's time window is approaching and sending a reminder will help people stay on track. Emailing participants can serve the dual purpose of identifying any problems and offering a gentle reminder that they are enrolled in the study.

Nothing beats checking in face to face to encourage higher response rates. Researchers commonly find that response rates rise in the days before an in-person check-in (e.g., Silvia et al., 2013). Compliance rates aside, meeting midstudy provides a chance to troubleshoot devices, collect new data (e.g., lab tasks), answer questions, give a midstudy incentive, and build rapport and goodwill (Hektner et al., 2007). If you don't meet at the conclusion of the study, you should develop an end-of-study message to thank people for taking part in your project, explain any steps they should take (e.g., uninstalling an app from their smartphone), and describe information about incentives or compensation.

Many researchers end up tailoring check-ins to each participant. If you can monitor participant behavior, you can identify participants who are not following instructions or have low response rates. A targeted reminder or nudge can reveal tech problems and raise study engagement. These targeted check-ins can be especially useful when people's compensation depends on their compliance (e.g., people must complete at least 5 surveys to receive research credit; everyone who completes at least 75% of surveys is entered in a raffle; for every 10 surveys completed, people earn an additional $5). For example, a study may enter people who complete at least 25 surveys out of 40 in one week of participation into a raffle. You could check response rates on Day 2 of participation and contact people who don't appear to be on track to qualify for the raffle (e.g., those with fewer than 5 completed surveys) to encourage participation. On Day 4 of participation, you may contact all participants regarding their progress toward the raffle—are they on track to qualify? Regardless of how you decide to check in with your participants, keep track of your communication with them for the sake of record-keeping, troubleshooting, and eventual data cleaning (Chapter 6) and publication (Chapter 8).

It can be tempting to take an "out of sight, out of mind" approach to conducting a daily life study, but tending the garden is vital for a successful project. Keeping track of all the moving parts of the study can be quite time intensive, more than newcomers expect. To keep things running smoothly, make sure to (a) monitor participant response rates and behavior, (b) check in with people during data collection, and (c) keep track of *everything*. Blocking off a chunk of time each day (~30–60 minutes, depending on the scale of the study) to check on the system, record any new information about participant activity, and send check-in emails will make this all manageable.

IMPROVING RESPONSE RATES AND DATA QUALITY

Your participants won't respond to every signal, so your response rate will fall short of 100%. Perfection is thus out, but what would a good response rate be? There's no one-size-fits-all heuristic for good response rates. Every study has different signaling designs, data collection systems, survey contents, research domains, and populations of interest. By understanding the causes of nonresponse, we can craft our data collection methods to promote higher response rates. Many factors that predict nonresponse—such as participant personality traits, clinical disorders, or momentary moods (Rintala et al., 2019; Silvia et al., 2013)—are outside our control. But, as intervention researchers put it, some factors are potentially modifiable, so we can craft our data collection plans to get closer to 100%.

Survey Factors

Researchers can improve responding by making their surveys livable (Black et al., 2012). One surefire way to destroy the goodwill of your participants is to bombard them with long surveys at inconvenient times. When deciding what the data collection period will look like, pay careful attention to your sampling window (i.e., when people will be sent surveys and how frequently). Is this when people are likely to be awake? Does it capture the times when the events of interest are likely to be happening? People won't answer surveys when they're sleeping (McLean et al., 2017) and won't be thrilled if they're signaled at times that don't make sense (e.g., asking what they ate for dinner at 2:00 p.m.).

Many studies allow participants to set their own sampling windows. For a 12-hour window, for example, some participants will choose 8:00 a.m. to 8:00 p.m., and others will choose 12:00 noon to midnight. This ensures that the signals are sent during times that the participants think are reasonable for their lifestyle. If participants can mute the signaling device (e.g., their own smartphone), you can use a wide sampling window (e.g., 6:00 a.m.–midnight), but encourage your participants to mute the device when sleeping and emphasize that you realize that some participants will never respond to the early morning or late night signals.

Another element that affects a survey's livability is its length. People will respond more frequently to shorter surveys (Intille et al., 2016). There's a delicate balance among the number of items per survey, surveys per day, and days in the study. Carefully evaluate whether each item is vital. If you are concerned about the length of your survey, see the tips for reducing survey length we discussed in Chapter 3.

The surveys and signals should be salient. Your response rate will be better if you can grab participants' attention at the right time. If you are using a random-interval or fixed-interval design, use several ways of notifying people when it's survey time. If you are using an app, this could involve having an auditory notification in addition to a visual app notification appear on the phone—an auditory signal appears to boost response rates (Srinivas et al., 2019). If the signaling and data collection systems are separate (e.g., a watch alarm as a signal to complete a paper survey), make sure the signaling mechanism will be noticeable to participants. Use redundant signals when possible. To remind people of their end-of-day diary, for example, you can send an email with the survey link and also text the link to participants' phones.

Salience is a unique issue in event-based designs. Participants can forget to complete a survey when a target behavior occurs, so compliance can decay over the course of a project. For instance, Wray et al. (2016) asked participants to initiate a survey when beginning to drink or use drugs. During days when drinking or drug use were indicated on a separate daily diary survey, an event-contingent survey was initiated only 64% of the time. Sending periodic reminders about these event-contingent surveys will make participants more likely to remember to complete them.

Study Factors

Many factors related to your overall study design can influence participant response rates. The factor that has received the most attention is the data collection system: pencil-and-paper surveys versus smartphone apps versus PDAs versus IVR versus texting. In general, electronic data collection systems show higher compliance rates than pencil-and-paper methods (e.g., Berkman et al., 2014; Stone et al., 2002), and participants find surveys easier to complete electronically (Berkman et al., 2014; Laughland & Kvavilashvili, 2018). We suspect that response rates are higher when participants use their own devices instead of a loaned device because they're motivated to keep their device charged and close at hand as they move throughout their days (see Chapter 4). If you are interested in studying effects over time, electronic methods have many advantages—people complete surveys closer to the signal (Berkman et al., 2014) and can't falsify the time stamp on their response (Stone et al., 2002). In addition, people often forget to bring paper surveys with them—in one study, 35% of participants forgot their surveys on at least one day (Laughland & Kvavilashvili, 2018).

Less work has directly compared electronic methods, but PDAs that allow brisk responding via touchscreens result in higher response rates than IVR systems, which are much slower (Burgin et al., 2012). You may not have the resources to use the fanciest smartphone app, but using online survey software over pencil-and-paper surveys will improve your response rates and data quality.

Time is a second factor that affects response rates. People tend to respond less as the study goes on (Ono et al., 2019; Phillips et al., 2014; Rintala et al., 2019; Tyler & Olson, 2018; Yang et al., 2019), and some studies have found that they respond more frequently on weekdays instead of weekends (Rintala et al., 2019), which are less structured and devoted to leisure activities. You can't control the passage of time, but you can create procedures to counteract these temporal trends. Checking in with participants will boost participant responding.

A midstudy in-person visit will increase responding (Burgin et al., 2012), but check-ins can also be done with texts, phone calls, and email. Contacting participants who aren't responding and praising participants for their consistent survey completion are well worth the effort (Tyler & Olson, 2018). To combat day-of-week effects, you can collect data in cohorts that start on the same day. Getting each cohort started on a Thursday (e.g., Reis et al., 2000), for example, prevents a confounding of the study day (e.g., the third day of data collection) with the week day (e.g., Saturday). Any day-of-week effects are thus held constant across participants.

CONCLUSION

The process of planning and collecting data is intricate, time consuming, and often frustrating for newcomers to daily life methods. In this chapter we have provided recommendations for gearing up for data collection and suggested ways to maintain good data quality. Pretesting everything and keeping detailed records of protocols, surveys, and participant responding are the cornerstones of a well-executed daily life study. Once you've survived data collection for your first study, it's time to sift through the mountains of responses you've collected, the focus of our next chapter.

6 CLEANING AND PROCESSING YOUR DATA

Much like humans, data files enter the world confused and unruly. All modes of research require wrangling, cleaning, checking, and preparing the data for analysis. Daily life data in their raw form are particularly messy, so you'll need to scrub them clean so that they're presentable in public (McCabe et al., 2012). This chapter describes how to get your data ready for analysis. We start by examining common quality issues in daily life data, such as low response rates, random responding, "clicking through," and widespread missingness. We then describe how to go from multiple raw data files to a single, multilevel analytic file and discuss ways to flag surveys and participants that are likely "screen outs."

ORGANIZING YOUR DATA

Heave a sigh of relief, do a happy dance, and take a little too much pleasure deleting your reminder to check in with participants—data collection is over. Once you've wrapped up data collection, it's time to sift and sort through the mountains of responses your participants have generated.

---

https://doi.org/10.1037/0000236-006
Researching Daily Life: A Guide to Experience Sampling and Daily Diary Methods, by P. J. Silvia and K. N. Cotter
Copyright © 2021 by the American Psychological Association. All rights reserved.

Taking Stock of Your Files

Before jumping to cleaning and merging your data files, double-check that your data look like they should. If you piloted your project carefully (see Chapter 5), you shouldn't see any surprises, but a little perfectionism goes a long way. Explore the responses to the items you asked participants. Are responses recoded if they are supposed to be? Some data collection systems don't come with automated recoding, so take note of which variables will need to be recoded. Are the response ranges correct? If several of your items use a Likert scale that ranges from 1 to 7, for example, verify that all recorded responses are within that range and that there aren't any impossible values (e.g., 0). How does the system handle missing responses? Some systems will leave cells blank, but others use a designated value (e.g., 99, NA, MISSING).

These data checks are things you probably are already doing and have pretested with your system (see Chapter 5), but there can occasionally be some quirks with data collection systems. Oftentimes, your collection system will get patched or updated while you are collecting data. These updates won't usually affect what your data file looks like, but it is possible that features related to automated recoding processes or how missing responses are denoted have changed since your pretesting. It's also possible that the devices participants are using will have installed software updates during data collection—these device updates could also interact with the data collection system and alter how responses are recorded. As a result, it is wise to take a little extra time and care to double-check your daily life data files.

In addition to survey responses, your data files will include many variables that your system automatically includes. This information will usually include the date and time of the submission and an identification number or code for the participant or individual response. Some systems will also provide more detailed information about each response—you might see what type of device each response was completed on, the geolocation of the response submission, or the time the signal was sent to participants. It's rare that this information will work its way into your analyses, but it may be useful when combining your data files or troubleshooting problems.

The information most commonly used for compiling data files is the system's participant identification number and the time stamp of the survey submission. Nevertheless, it's good practice to create and preserve a raw master file (Berenson, 2018), both as an archival file and as a backup should your data cleaning and wrangling go horribly awry.

Cleaning up Your Data File

Once you've confirmed your data file has all the expected parts, it's time to scrub and polish it. Just like in your standard lab study, there will be some responses to recode, variables to rename, and scale scores to calculate before your data file is ready for analysis. Cleaning up these aspects of your daily life data files will function like cleaning up your lab data files. In daily life research, however, you'll usually have a portfolio of data files you'll need to clean up: at least one file for daily life survey responses and probably files for between-person measures (e.g., demographics, surveys, lab tasks, brain scans). As a general rule, it's wise to clean these files separately before merging them so you can double-check that any changes you are making are done properly. At this stage, it can be tempting to take care of any necessary exclusions (e.g., removing participants for low response rates or omitting individual surveys on the basis of screening procedures), but for daily life work these are best saved until your analytic file is nearly ready.

A special element of cleaning and preparing daily life data is deciding how to represent time in the data file. At a minimum, your data set should have the clock time and date for each sampled occasion, including for "missed beeps" when participants didn't respond, so that time can be calculated many ways. Here are some common ways you could represent time:

1. **Serial order.** You can represent serial order, counting up as the study progresses. The most common index is the serial order of the *signal*, ranging from 0 to k. Another is the serial order of the *response*, ranging from the participant's first response to the final one. These seemingly similar time indexes will vary: The serial order of the signal is the same for all participants, but the serial order of responses varies. Some people will have completed their eighth survey on the eighth beep, for example, but others will have completed their eighth survey on Beep 10, 12, or 15. A variable marking the serial order of the signal is a useful predictor when exploring reactivity (e.g., whether measuring the construct alters the scores) and response rate trends (e.g., how response rates changed over time; see Chapter 3).

2. **Calendar days.** In many studies, specific days of the week are uniquely interesting, such as studies of "blue Monday" effects on mood (Larsen & Kasimatis, 1990), young adults' heavy drinking on Fridays and Saturdays (Kuntsche & Cooper, 2010), and how greater autonomy on Saturdays and Sundays affects mood and well-being (Ryan et al., 2010). In other studies, coding the day of the week allows exploring circaseptal trends (i.e., 7-day cycles; Larsen & Kasimatis, 1990) or contrasting weekend

days with weekdays (Liu & West, 2016). You thus might have a binary variable (e.g., weekend day vs. weekday) or a variable denoting the day of the week. (When coding and reporting, note that cultures vary in whether Saturday, Sunday, or Monday is considered the first day of the week.)

3. **Time intervals.** In fixed-interval designs, the time intervals between occasions are, needless to say, fixed, but in random-interval designs the time between beeps varies. Coding the time intervals between occasions—such as how many minutes elapsed between two beeps in an experience sampling study or how long since enrollment in the study—is useful for analyses that account for time dependence. Estimating within-person variability and volatility in emotional instability, for example, requires knowing the temporal distance between responses (Ebner-Priemer et al., 2009).

4. **Durations.** Many studies focus on how long it took for something to happen. Elapsed time—often called *time-to-event* or *duration*—will be familiar to researchers versed in survival analysis, which examines how long it takes for an event to happen, if it happens at all (Rathbun et al., 2013). Studies of smoking, for example, might explore how many minutes elapsed since waking before someone smoked their first cigarette of the day, if they smoked at all. Defining the event that "starts the clock" is critical for analyzing durations. A common "time zero" event is the start of the day, usually defined by waking time, but it might be the start of the workday (e.g., 9:00 a.m.) or the onset of a focal behavior (e.g., exercising, injecting insulin, arguing with a spouse).

5. **Lagged time.** A serial index of time can be expanded to explore time-lagged effects. In traditional longitudinal models with only a handful of time points, for example, researchers use the family of panel models to estimate concurrent effects and lagged effects across the time points (T. D. Little, 2013). In daily life studies, a common use of lags is to explore carryover effects across occasions, such as whether fruit and vegetable consumption yesterday predicts well-being today, controlling for yesterday's well-being (Conner et al., 2015).

Restructuring Your Data Files

The final step in organizing your data is creating the data file used for analysis. You'll likely have a few different cleaned data files—some for the daily life part and some for between-person tasks and surveys. When combining data files from lab research, you are typically pooling data files with the same variables (e.g., the same personality survey was given on 20 different devices, yielding 20 files) or pooling data files with at least some unique variables (e.g., combining a demographic survey, response times to cognitive tasks, and Big Five personality scores, all linked by a shared ID variable). In both cases, the typical lab or survey study ends up with a data file in *wide format*: Each participant has a single row in our data file, with scores for the any variables in different columns.

An analytic file for a daily life project, however, will look quite different. Most software you will use for analyses will require your file to be in *long format*, not wide format. In long format, participants will have multiple rows of data; each row represents a unique daily life response. Figure 6.1 shows what the same hypothetical data would look like in wide and long formats. In wide format, participants will have only one row of data, but each daily life item will have multiple columns. For example, if you ask people about their mood in a daily diary for 10 days, the item "Happy" will appear as 10 different columns, one for each of the diaries. In long format, participants will have several rows of data. The scores for your daily life items will vary from row to row, and the scores for between-person variables measured only once (e.g., age, scores on a personality scale) will be duplicated on each row.

We recommend flipping your daily life data files into long format before combining them with your between-person data files to create your final mega-file. It can take a few tries to get the file into the proper format, so you'll save time and avoid disastrous mistakes by restructuring before merging. When creating your long file, one decision you'll face is whether to include rows for missed observations. Figure 6.1 shows both forms. One option, shown in the middle of Figure 6.1, includes rows only for completed surveys. If someone didn't respond to that day's survey, the row is omitted. The other option is to create a row for each occasion regardless. If someone didn't respond to the survey, the survey scores are obviously missing, but any other variables (e.g., the date, day of week, and occasion number) are still coded. Adding rows for missed surveys is helpful for some kinds of temporal analyses and for exploring predictors of missingness. If there aren't any temporal analyses planned, omitting these rows is fine.

Restructuring a data file from wide to long is something your software does for you, not something you do by hand with error-prone copying and transposing. Any software package worth using for daily life analyses has automated functions for complex data restructuring. You might need to consult a book, read a tutorial, or ask an anonymous Belgian postdoc on a

FIGURE 6.1. Example of Wide Versus Long Data File Formats for a Hypothetical Daily Diary Study

1. Wide Format

Participant	Age	Date.1	Happy.1	Date.2	Happy.2	Date.3	Happy.3
1	19	4/1/2020	5	4/3/2020	4	NA	NA
2	23	4/1/2020	1	NA	NA	NA	NA
3	21	4/2/2020	6	4/2/2020	5	4/3/2020	6

2. Long Format (Missed Days Omitted)

Participant	Age	Date	Happy	Occasion
1	19	4/1/2020	5	0
1	19	4/3/2020	4	2
2	23	4/1/2020	1	0
3	21	4/1/2020	6	0
3	21	4/2/2020	5	1
3	21	4/3/2020	6	2

3. Long Format (Missed Days Included)

Participant	Age	Date	Happy	Occasion
1	19	4/1/2020	5	0
1	19	4/2/2020	NA	1
1	19	4/3/2020	4	2
2	23	4/1/2020	1	0
2	23	4/2/2020	NA	1
2	23	4/3/2020	NA	2
3	21	4/1/2020	6	0
3	21	4/2/2020	5	1
3	21	4/3/2020	6	2

Note. In the wide file (top panel), each daily diary response is a column. Notice how, because of missing data, scores for the same variable might not reflect the same occasion. Scores for "Happy.2" represent the second survey someone completed, and the two fictional participants completed it on different days. In the long file (middle and bottom panels), each diary response is a row. Scores for between-person variables (e.g., "Age") are duplicated. An "Occasion" variable has been added to index the day of the study, ranging from Time 0 to k. The first long file omits rows for the days without responses; the second long file includes rows for missed days. Including omitted rows is useful for some kinds of analyses. NA = not available.

stats discussion board, but once you understand how to restructure your data you can archive your scripts and syntax to save time later. One way to check that this process went smoothly is to look at your ID variables. In your one-shot lab session file, each ID should occur only once and have only one row; in your daily life file each ID will occur multiple times, one row for each survey. Making sure that each lab file ID occurs only once and that each daily life file ID occurs the same number of times in the restructured file and the original file is probably the best way to catch any restructuring issues.

Merging Your Data Files

Once your individual data files are properly structured, it's time to merge them into a single mega-file that contains all the project's variables. Merging all your data can be the most daunting part of cleaning and preparing your data. As always, retain and archive raw forms of the individual files in case you need to revert and start anew. Here are the steps to merge your data files and check that things went smoothly (see Exhibit 6.1 for a summary).

1. **Check your ID variables.** The ID you use to differentiate participants is the linchpin of this process. As we argued in Chapter 5, you need a foolproof way of linking a participant's records across all modes of data collection, from paper diaries to clinical interviews to MRI scans

---

EXHIBIT 6.1. Creating Your Analytic Data File

Going from several raw data files—some containing lab data, some containing daily life data—into a single analytic file can be daunting. Here is a summary of the steps:

1. **Check your ID variables.** Verify that your ID variable makes sense for each file, such as examining daily life files and lab files (in which IDs should be used only once) for duplicate IDs or daily life files. Ensure that this ID variable has the same name in each file.

2. **Additional merging information.** If you are using any additional variables for matching (e.g., date, device, location), ensure that they have the same variable name and format.

3. **Matching cases and merging files.** Next, you need to tell your software how you want the merge to go. Specify the variables that should be used for matching cases, that you are interested in adding variables (not new cases), that all matching cases should be retained, and that all non-matching cases should be retained.

4. **Did it work?** The last step is to do a quality check on the merge. Did the variables get added? Do you have the number of data rows you expected? Are the missing data flags correct? Do the descriptive statistics from the new file match the stats from the raw data files?

to smartphone surveys. This identifier should already be included in all files. Scour each file for any typos or issues in the ID variables. In your non–daily life files, in which each participant will have only one row, are there any duplicate IDs? Are there any implausible IDs (e.g., if there are 150 participants but you have an ID of "220")? In your daily life files, checking IDs can be a bit trickier because people will have different numbers of rows. You can easily check for any implausible IDs, but checking if the same ID was accidentally used for multiple participants can be a bit trickier. This is one reason for using some redundancy when creating ID variables (see Chapter 5). Relying on these tricks, such as using two methods of identifying participants, will minimize any mismatching of responses. If your ID contains letters (e.g., names), make sure capitalization is consistent—*Lauren* and *lauren* may not be treated equally by your software and could create issues during merging. (Automatically converting all text to uppercase, much like a social media rant about cats, can save time.) Finally, ensure the ID variable has the same variable name and the same format across all data files. Some software won't allow you to merge files if the ID in one file is listed as a numeric variable in one file but as a character or string variable in others.

- **Working with electronic system identifiers.** If you are using an electronic data collection system (e.g., an app) that generates its own unique, internal identifier for participants (e.g., a long string of letters and numbers), you probably have included a survey the research team completes that allows you to match your own ID for each participant with the system-generated identifier (see Chapter 5). In most systems, the responses for the identifier survey and the responses for your daily life survey will be stored in separate files. Before combining your daily life and non–daily life files, you will need to merge the files containing your identifier and the daily life survey responses. To do this, follow the process described in Step 3 ("Matching cases and merging files") to create a finalized daily life data file. Instead of matching on your ID variable, you'll match using the system-generated identifier.

2. **Additional information for merging.** In some cases, you may have a few different daily life surveys that are related and need to be matched to one another as well. A common example is when studies combine within-day experience sampling with an end-of-day survey. Your system will yield different data files for the two surveys, and you'll need to match and merge them so that you'll know which within-day responses occurred on the same day as your end-of-day survey. To do this, you'll need to prepare additional factors for matching, such as the date. If you use the

date or time as a matching factor, ensure that they're formatted the same way in all files (e.g., MM/DD/YYYY vs. MM/DD/YY vs. DD/MM/YYYY vs. DD/MM/YY). As before, check that variables used to match responses during the merge have the same structure and format.

3. **Matching cases and merging files.** Once you've verified that your data files are in proper shape, it's time to merge them to create a single, multilevel file that you will use for your analyses. Matching cases and merging files can be a finicky process. We urge you to actually read the software manual or a tutorial before randomly clicking buttons and typing code. Depending on the software you are using, the command names and terminology will differ, but the basic functions of these commands will be the same. To complete the merge, you'll complete four steps.

    - First, specify your *key variables* for matching—this will usually be your ID variable that distinguishes participants, but you may also wish to match cases on additional factors, such as dates.

    - Second, specify that you want to add *additional variables*, not additional cases or participants. Although your final data file will have more rows than your original non–daily life file, your primary interest is in adding variables (e.g., daily life variables) to the lab-based variables already in your data file.

    - Third, specify how *duplicate matches* should be handled. In daily life research, each participant will have many rows of daily life data but only one row of between-person variables (e.g., age, personality scale scores), so we need to make sure all responses are retained in the merge. To do so, you'll need to tell your software that it should retain all matching cases in the final file. Ideally, the between-person scores are duplicated across a participant's rows (see Figure 6.1).

    - Fourth and finally, specify how to handle *nonmatching cases*. Nonmatching cases occur when a value of your key variables used for matching appears in one file but not the other. The most common case of this in daily life work is when a participant completes your between-person measures but doesn't complete any daily life surveys, or vice versa. To obtain all available scores, instruct your software to include any instances of nonmatching cases in your final data file.

4. **Did it work?** The final step in creating your analytic file is confirming that the merge went as intended. Verify that you have the same number of daily responses in the merged file as in the individual files. The two

files should have the same number of rows unless some participants did not submit any daily life responses, which will add extra rows containing these participants' non–daily life information. Next, make sure all participants made it through the merge—are all the IDs in the original files still listed after the merge? Usually, your data file containing non–daily life information can be considered the "official" source of who all participants are. A common issue that occurs during merging is the exclusion of participants who are absent in one of the files (e.g., people who didn't complete any daily life surveys).

One method to check whether the merging went correctly is to generate frequency tables and calculate basic descriptive statistics. To make sure the daily life responses merged correctly, get descriptive statistics for your daily life variables in the individual file and recalculate them in the merged file. These values should match—even if a few participants didn't complete the daily life surveys, they will show up as "missing" on these variables. If the values don't match, this may mean that some of your daily life responses didn't make it through the merge or were duplicated. To make sure all non–daily life information merged correctly, generate frequency distribution tables for the ID variable in the non–daily life files and the merged file. The frequency of the ID variables will be different, but the categories (i.e., the ID values) should be the same in the table. If these don't match, a participant was likely excluded in the merge. No one should have missing data on the ID variable, so if there are missing values after the merge, something went awry.

ASSESSING DATA QUALITY

Now that your data are all in one place, it's time to take stock of what you have. The coarse daily life data need some sanding and polishing prior to analysis, so you should think through two issues. First, how much data are missing, and what does the pattern of missingness tell you? Second, if you believe that some responses should be filtered, what are your criteria for screening out surveys and participants?

Missingness Is Widespread and Messy

Most behavioral research methods will yield at least some missing observations, people being the flaky and contrary creatures that they are, but daily life methods yield data sets with missingness that is widespread and messy. Time-based designs usually yield extensive missingness, particularly when

TABLE 6.1. An Example of Missing Data Patterns for a Hypothetical Study With Two Time Points

Pattern	Time 1	Time 2	% of Sample
1	X	X	70
2	X		30

Note. X indicates observed data; an empty cell indicates missing data.

people are intensively sampled at random intervals. And the patterns of missingness—the unique combinations of observed and missing scores—are diverse and complex. Examining patterns of missingness can yield insight into why scores are missing (McKnight et al., 2007). In a two-time point study, for example, you usually see only two patterns of missing data; Table 6.1 shows a hypothetical example. Most people have observations at both time points, but some people provide data for only the first time point and then drop out.

Daily life studies have many patterns, some eccentric and peculiar, so they tend to have what McKnight et al. (2007) called "messy missing data" (p. 109). In missing data theory, missingness is classified with three mechanisms (R. J. A. Little & Rubin, 1987): (a) missing completely at random (MCAR; when missingness is truly random), (b) missing at random (MAR; missingness is correlated with observed scores but not missing ones), and (c) missing not at random (MNAR; missingness is correlated with scores on the variable itself). In the messy missingness typical of daily life data, for example, missing scores from a single participant may be MCAR (e.g., a one-time tech problem), MAR (e.g., skipping surveys early in the day), or MNAR (e.g., skipping items about drinking during periods of heavy drinking) at different occasions across the study. The challenge of missingness, then, is not simply that it is pervasive but that it is messily patterned and often obscure in its origins. Understanding these statistical mechanisms can guide analytic decisions, but in real-world data sets all three mechanisms can be at work (McKnight et al., 2007).

Researchers should seek to understand why scores are missing so they can reduce missingness by means of design features (see Chapter 5). Using Cattell's (1966) classic data box as a heuristic, McKnight et al. (2007) proposed unpacking missingness into dimensions. For a daily diary or experience-sampling study, a project has three dimensions on which data can be missing:

1. **Missing by person.** A participant's daily life data can be wholly missing. This isn't a common pattern, but many studies will have a few participants

who provided no rows of diary data because they encountered tech calamities (e.g., for obscure reasons, their smartphone failed to show surveys) or they decided to ignore the beeps.

2. **Missing by item.** Like cross-sectional surveys, some daily surveys will have missing data for some items within a completed survey. In daily life data, missed items happen when participants skip items—deliberately or accidentally—or stop completing the survey midway. Skipping creates patches of missed items; stopping creates complete data for the early survey items and missing data for the remaining ones.

3. **Missing by beep.** All data for a single occasion—a beep in an experience sampling study or a day in a daily diary study—can be wholly missing. Beep-wise missingness is by far the most common dimension of missingness. It reflects all the reasons why people might miss a survey: encountering tech problems, being caught at an unsafe time, failing to notice a survey, and deciding not to respond (see Chapter 5).

Identifying "Screen Outs"

Just as cross-sectional studies need rules for excluding participants from data analysis, daily life studies need guidelines for screening out data. A wrinkle, however, is that the intensive, repeated quality of daily life data creates two kinds of exclusions: We can exclude beeps (i.e., omit a participant's scores from one of their occasions but not from the others) or we can exclude participants (i.e., exclude a participant's data entirely).

Excluding Beeps

Just as you may exclude individual trials in behavioral tasks because of quality concerns (e.g., abnormal response times; Ratcliff, 1993), you should evaluate whether any individual survey responses raise quality concerns. For some participants, responses from some occasions should probably be dropped and treated as missing. Unfortunately, there are not yet standard procedures or best practices for screening out single occasions, and the issue of beep-wise exclusion gets surprisingly little attention. Here are some factors that you can examine to evaluate the quality of responses:

1. **Were instructions followed?** In some cases, a survey must be completed within a specific time window (e.g., between 3:00 and 5:00 p.m., before 9:00 a.m., or within 15 minutes of smoking a cigarette). Unless your system prevents it, participants will submit surveys at invalid times, so be sure to scrutinize the time stamps. If a response falls outside the valid

window, it should be excluded. Similarly, event-contingent responses should be completed only when the event of interest has occurred. If people indicate the specified event did not occur but still recorded a response, it should obviously be excluded.

2. **When should I drop a single survey?** Inattentive and careless responding are common reasons for dropping a single survey. Participants who were generally good-natured about competing the surveys might occasionally "click through" a survey just to get it over with. In cross-sectional surveys, researchers have many tools for catching such patterns (Maniaci & Rogge, 2014; McKibben & Silvia, 2016), such as including directed response options (e.g., "Please select *Strongly Disagree*") or infrequency scales with items people shouldn't endorse (e.g., "I sometimes eat cement"). These tricks are less practical for daily life surveys. Every item counts in a daily life survey, and participants get irked when surveys are long (Eisele et al., 2020). Including attention-check items occasionally (e.g., every fourth occasion, on average) would be worthwhile if your system affords it, but including them at every beep would grate on your participants.

3. **How long did it take to complete the survey?** A key marker of potentially invalid beeps is how long it took participants to complete a survey. Electronic data collection systems typically time-stamp when someone began a survey and when it was submitted to the system—calculate the difference between these two values and look for unusual values. Surveys with unusually short times (e.g., 20 seconds for a 35-item survey) likely indicate that people weren't reading your items. Surveys with unusually long times (e.g., 30 minutes for a 10-item survey) suggest that people didn't complete the survey in one sitting. Because we're often interested in momentary, fleeting experiences, surveys that weren't completed in one sitting don't capture what we're studying. Set some a priori rules (i.e., inclusion criteria) for judging whether a survey was too fast or too slow.

4. **Do the responses "look" valid?** Examining people's response patterns can detect "clicking through" and otherwise random responding. One method is to examine response patterns for lack of variability (i.e., "straightlining"; Y. Kim et al., 2019; Zhang & Conrad, 2014). Sometimes people will open your survey only to provide the same response to every question. It is possible that people do feel similarly for all items, but usually people give varying scores. Looking for this type of responding, in concert with completion time (Y. Kim et al., 2019), is one way to

identify likely low-quality responses. Computing the standard deviation across a set of items will flag beeps with little or no variability for further inspection.

An alternate approach to identifying random responding is to examine a collection of items for which there should be variable scores. For example, if you have a pool of positive and negative affect items measured on a 1–5 scale, you would be skeptical of someone who clicked "5" for all items: Someone who is very happy is rarely also very calm, bored, and angry. Looking at response patterns to determine data quality can be tricky and shouldn't be the only method you use to decide whether to exclude a beep.

Excluding Participants

The other decision you'll need to make is whether there are any participants who should be excluded wholesale from the analyses. Like in your traditional lab-based or survey research, you probably have some standard guidance for determining exclusions based on careless and inattentiveness—these may include aberrant behavior in the lab (e.g., sleeping), poor performance on measures designed to capture inattentive or inconsistent responding, or information that came to light during or after the study (e.g., self-reported carelessness). In other cases, participants will be fully excluded for reasons unrelated to data quality, such as changes in clinical symptoms that make continued participation unsafe, withdrawal of consent, or acquiring information that would render someone ineligible (e.g., in a study restricted to moderate social drinkers, someone's daily diary data might reveal serious alcohol abuse). These sorts of exclusions are sensible and can still apply when performing data quality checks for daily life projects with a lab-based component.

The most widespread and most controversial criterion for excluding participants in daily life research is response rates. To give some color to this issue, Figure 6.2 illustrates the distributions of response rates for a few studies. It is common to find researchers excluding participants who do not meet some compliance threshold, such as completing a specified percentage of all beeps, and using such a method is recommended in most guidance (e.g., Trull & Ebner-Priemer, 2020). Again, these exclusion criteria should be determined and documented before data collection. But there is little consistency in what is used as an "acceptable" compliance threshold, and these thresholds vary widely between studies. In an experience sampling study with up to 70 possible responses, for example, researchers might require a minimum number of responses (e.g., 5, 10, 20), require a minimum percentage of responses (e.g., 10%, 25%), seek a certain coverage level

FIGURE 6.2. Examples of Real Response Rate Distributions From Experience Sampling and Daily Diary Projects

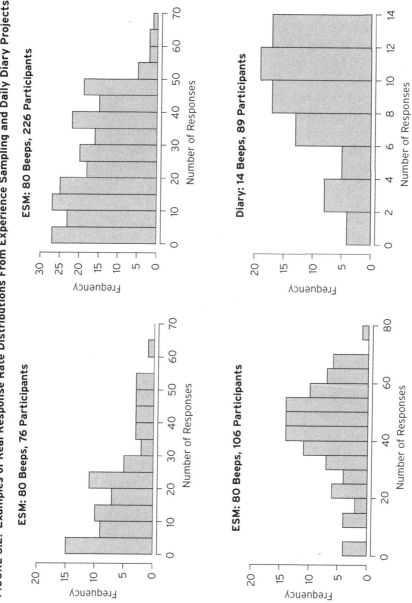

Note. The response rate data are from Cotter and Silvia (2020; top left panel), Cotter (2020; top right panel), Nusbaum et al. (2014; bottom left panel), and Eddington and Foxworth (2012; bottom right panel). ESM = experience sampling method.

(e.g., an average of at least two responses per day), or apply a bottom-up rule (e.g., finding a natural "joint" at the low end of the response rate distribution). The argument for using compliance thresholds is that as the degree of missingness increases, our estimated effects may be less reliable or our models may not be able to adequately handle high sparseness (e.g., 70% of beeps missing). At very high levels of missingness (e.g., 90%), it is likely that the participants were signaling their desire to withdraw from participating.

Another school of thought recommends against excluding participants on the basis of response rates (Jacobson, 2020). This approach points out that when we exclude people with lower response rates, we are probably biasing our sample because response rates are associated with individual-difference factors. Participant characteristics, unsurprisingly, shape response rates. Typically, women (Mackesy-Amiti & Boodram, 2018; Rintala et al., 2019), older participants (Ono et al., 2019; Rintala et al., 2019), and healthy or nonclinical control participants (Jones et al., 2019; Rintala et al., 2019; Santangelo et al., 2017) have higher response rates. When we omit people with low response rates we are often excluding people with relatively more severe symptoms and volatile daily lives—in many cases, the people we most want to study. For some projects, the population of interest is hard to reach and expensive to recruit—such as studies of injection drug users (Mackesy-Amiti & Boodram, 2018), homeless youth (Tyler & Olson, 2018), and men who have sex with men (Wray et al., 2016)—so a strong justification would be needed to exclude an expensive participant for falling under an arbitrary threshold.

We once again emphasize that prevention is the cure for missing data problems (McKnight et al., 2007), including the dilemma of what to do about excluding participants with too few responses. Researchers should not be fatalistic about response rates. As we have described throughout this book, a human-friendly sampling design and survey (see Chapters 2 and 3), combined with a system for tracking compliance, checking in during data collection, and offering incentives for engagement (Chapter 5), will increase your response rates. If you have a lot of participants with worryingly low compliance, your first task is to try to understand the causes of poor engagement so you can get better compliance in your next study. If necessary, you can selectively target participants who are at risk of poor responding (e.g., adding an extra check-in per week or offering additional cash incentives) to raise the floor of your response rate distribution (Silvia et al., 2013).

Nevertheless, you'll need to arrive at a decision about excluding participants with low response rates. Including everyone is a legitimate, defensible option (Jacobson, 2020). Researchers who advocate for including everyone point out that full-information maximum likelihood and multiple-imputation techniques can appropriately handle missing daily life data.

Consistent with the broader simulation literature on missing data (Enders, 2010), simulation work shows that these tools provide parameter estimates with low bias in the kinds of models used for daily life data (e.g., Jacobson et al., 2019; Ji et al., 2018), including complex models dealing with time lags (Jacobson et al., 2019). But if you believe that some participants essentially didn't participate and ought to be dropped, you might consider a cutoff of five responses, which we think balances retaining most participants with omitting the most seriously disengaged ones. Bolger and Laurenceau (2013) defined an intensive longitudinal study as one that has at least five time points, based on the amount of information needed to adequately specify a within-person model, so a cutoff of five responses strikes us as appropriately low and defensible.

CONCLUSION

Cleaning and preparing your data for analysis can be an ordeal even for simple studies, so be prepared for the drama and spectacle of wrangling the data from your first daily life project. Altogether, the first time you clean and prepare daily life data could take you a couple of days to figure out how your statistical software handles these processes, write code or syntax to automate the procedures, and check to make sure everything went as it should. As you become more familiar with these steps you will become more efficient and can recycle your code, so you'll do this in hours instead of days.

In this chapter we have described how to get your data into analytic shape and considered issues involved in evaluating data quality and making exclusions. There are many ways that cleaning, merging, and working with multilevel data files can go wonky, so triple-checking all your procedures is essential. And once you have wrangled your data into shape, it's time to move on to everyone's favorite part: data analysis.

7
ANALYZING DAILY LIFE DATA

One of our undergraduate mentors had a sign in his office that said, "Don't start vast projects with half-vast ideas." (Say it aloud if you don't get it.) For daily life researchers, a less salty motto would be, "Don't collect what you can't analyze." Daily life projects yield data sets that are as large and unruly as a litter of Newfoundland puppies. You may already have the statistical training needed to analyze the data you plan to collect, but you may not. Although analyzing daily life data isn't too formidable, it does require going beyond the familiar terrain of ANOVA, multiple regression, and structural equation modeling.

Our goal in this chapter is to walk through the distinctive features of daily life data and point out some features that new researchers often don't notice. This chapter isn't a tutorial for analyzing daily life data. That would require a book of its own, and fortunately some fine ones have already been written (Bolger & Laurenceau, 2013; Nezlek, 2012). Our aim is to help you decide whether you already have the necessary stats chops, whether you should read a few books or take a workshop, or whether you should entrust this facet of the project to another member of your research team whose heart is warmed by two-level random-coefficient models.

---

https://doi.org/10.1037/0000236-007
Researching Daily Life: A Guide to Experience Sampling and Daily Diary Methods,
by P. J. Silvia and K. N. Cotter
Copyright © 2021 by the American Psychological Association. All rights reserved.

SOME PECULIAR QUALITIES OF DAILY LIFE DATA

Compared with the typical lab experiment or survey, daily life data have some peculiar and distinctive features. Here are the biggest quirks to understand so that you can steel yourself for the unruly data file your project will yield.

Some Participants Participate More

In a one-shot, cross-sectional survey, every participant provides roughly the same amount of data. Some people might skip some items or stop responding midway, but there isn't much variance in how much data someone contributed to the data set. A participant either has a row of data or not, so the range is 0 to 1. Ignoring the vagaries of partial missing data for now, this means that participants in the usual cross-sectional study all have the same weight and influence. To describe the sample, you can just average the rows.

In daily life data, however, some participants end up participating much more than others. Participants vary in how many surveys they complete, so some will contribute many more rows than others. The participants with the most responses invariably provide at least twice as many rows—if not 5 to 10 times as many—as participants with the fewest (see Chapter 6). Exhibit 7.1 describes a few reasons—some obvious, some subtle—why participants vary in their data rows.

Unequal participation has many implications for data analysis, but we'll note two serious ones here. First, we can't analyze each row as an independent observation as if each one were generated by a different participant. To understand why, consider a hypothetical data set of three people who reported their daily emotions in a 7-day diary study. Table 7.1 displays ratings for daily happiness (1 = *not at all happy*, 5 = *very happy*) for the three fictional participants. The first two participants responded only a few times, but the third responded all 7 days. The mean of the 11 observations ($M = 3.91$ out of 5.00) suggests a pretty happy sample. But this value is misleading because one happy participant contributed so much more data than the others. What we really have are two relatively grumpy participants ($Ms = 2.50$ and 3.00) and one exuberant one ($M = 4.57$). A disaggregated analysis will always mislead whenever some people contribute more data than others and vary in their means and variances.

Second, many statistical models require that each participant have the same number of observations. An off-the-shelf correlation and regression

> **EXHIBIT 7.1. Why Do Some Participants Have More Data Rows?**
>
> In event-based sampling designs, your participants will vary in how often they experience the focal event, such as completing a survey each time they smoke a cigarette, argue with a relationship partner, or have an episode of disordered eating. Variance in rows is mostly driven by true variability in how often people experience the event; the rest reflects variability in people's motivation to participate and thresholds for noticing an event (see Chapter 2). For these designs, then, variance in rows indicates that the study is working as it should. The design is revealing between-person differences in how often these events happen.
>
> In time-based sampling designs, variance in rows is mostly driven by participant nonresponse (see Chapter 5). A 3-week daily diary study, for example, should yield 21 responses per participant. Any number lower than that comes from participants not providing data for a day. The reasons are many, including reasons outside of participants' control: illness; power failures; natural disasters; and a multitude of tech problems, from system glitches to phones dropped in toilets. But the most common reasons are motivational, such as flaking for a day or dropping out of the study.
>
> Finally, some missed surveys reflect the inevitable flaws in sampling from a complex population of experiences. In sampling theory, the population that you wish to assess is empirically defined by your *sampling frame* (Henry, 1990; Silvia, 2020). A survey study of clinical psychology graduate students, for example, might have a sampling frame defined by a list of all graduate students currently enrolled in American Psychological Association–accredited PhD programs. When a sampling frame includes ineligible elements—the list might include a few nonclinical students and some students who dropped out—it is *overinclusive*, a common flaw.
>
> For daily life studies, we are sampling a subset of occasions from the population of daily life experiences. Occasionally, we will inadvertently seek to sample an occasion that falls outside the project's sampling frame of occasions. Nearly all studies, for example, are interested in occasions during the person's waking hours. If a survey signal is missed because someone slept in, that missed survey reflects *overinclusive* sampling—an attempt to assess an element outside the population of interest—not participant nonresponse. Likewise, population elements that cannot be sampled ethically are excluded from a sampling frame. When people ignore a survey signal because responding would be risky or harmful (e.g., while driving), the missed survey reflects overinclusive sampling instead of nonresponse.

analysis, for example, presumes that each person has an identical number of rows—one row, usually. Even many models designed for nested, interdependent observations, such as repeated-measures analysis of variance, require equal observations per participant. Disparate levels of participation thus require statistical models that can accommodate different participant-level sample sizes, such as the family of multilevel models (Nezlek, 2012).

Observations Are Nested and Nonindependent

Responses to daily life surveys are *nested* because each person provides a cluster of responses over time. In stats parlance, the repeated observations

TABLE 7.1. Hypothetical Data Illustrating the Effects of Unequal Participation

Participant	Occasion	Happiness rating
1	1	3
1	2	2
2	1	2
2	2	4
3	1	5
3	2	5
3	3	4
3	4	3
3	5	5
3	6	5
3	7	5

Note. Treating each row as if it were a participant gives a misleading view of the sample's levels of happiness. The disaggregated happiness score–the simple average of the 11 rows–is $M = 3.91$. But the three cluster means–the means for each participant–are 2.50, 3.00, and 4.57. The average cluster mean is 3.36, much lower than the disaggregated mean.

are nested within participants. When researchers talk about nested data, they describe it in terms of *levels*. Repeated daily diary data have two levels. The first is the within-person level: the level of repeated observations that vary within each participant, such as the dozens of happiness scores a person provided over a month. The second is the between-person level: the level of scores that don't vary across the study, such as a participant's personality traits, year of birth, or prestudy clinical status. Your within-person variables have many observations per person; your between-person variables have only one score per person. In generic terms, the within-person level is also called the *lower level* or *Level 1*, and the between-person level is called the *higher level* or *Level 2*. We'll use *within-person level* and *between-person level* because they are more intuitive when discussing intensive daily life designs.

When you collect nested data, you should expect the scores to be nonindependent. You can think of nonindependence in a couple ways:

1. For each participant, a given score is more likely to resemble his or her own scores than another participant's scores.

2. In a sample of independent observations, a particularly high score is equally likely to come from any of the participants, all else equal. But for nested data, a particularly high score is more likely to come from some participants—those participants with higher average scores—than others.

Table 7.2 illustrates nonindependence with real data from three participants in a daily diary study who rated their daily happiness on a scale that ranges from 1 to 7. When looking at their raw scores, you can see that some participants were usually happier than others. The mean of the 30 scores is 4.87, but some participants were, on average, more (Participant 1) or less (Participant 3) happy than the sample.

Nonindependence isn't all or none, so your scores can fall on a spectrum of interdependence. The degree of clustering is captured by the *intraclass correlation* (ICC). An ICC varies from 0 to 1 and indicates the degree of total variance that is at the between-person level. In the typical daily life study it would thus reflect the proportion of variance that is due to mean differences between people (e.g., the fact that people vary from each other in their average happiness) rather than variation within people (e.g., the fact that each person varies in happiness at least little from one day to another). An ICC is easy to compute by hand, but any software for multilevel modeling that is worth using will compute it for you.

ICCs are interesting in their own right to daily life researchers. Within-person variability—the fluctuations in moods, thoughts, and actions as people move through their environments during the day and throughout the week—is itself fascinating. Knowing how much a construct varies within people in their natural habitats tells you something important about it. In our own experience sampling research with university students, we commonly give surveys eight to 12 times daily for a week and ask about momentary emotional states and social activity. The ICC values for ratings of common emotions and subjective states—such as how happy, sad, worried, irritated, relaxed, or tired people are—usually range from .25 to .40, which are common in the broader literature of emotional experience in daily life. An ICC of .30 for happiness means that 30% of the variance in happiness is between people (some people just tend to be happier than others) but most of the variance, 70%, varies within people as part of the volatile ebbs and flows of daily emotion. Events that vary greatly within a day have even lower ICC values. Whether people happen to be alone at the time they're signaled, for example, usually has an ICC of around .20 in our samples. Whether people happen to be hearing music in their minds is even more variable within the day, with ICC values of around .15 (e.g., Cotter et al., 2019; Cotter & Silvia, 2017).

Beyond their inherent interestingness, ICCs are practical because they imply fruitful places for look for explaining variability. If an ICC is quite high (e.g., over .70), most of the variance is between people, so between-person predictors are more likely to be fertile. But if the ICCs are low (e.g., under .30),

TABLE 7.2. Example Responses for Daily Happiness for Three Participants

Day	Participant 1			Participant 2			Participant 3		
	Raw	Person mean centered	Grand mean centered	Raw	Person mean centered	Grand mean centered	Raw	Person mean centered	Grand mean centered
1	6	0.2	1.13	5	0	0.13	3	−0.8	−1.87
2	7	1.2	2.13	3	−2	−1.87	3	−0.8	−1.87
3	7	1.2	2.13	6	1	1.13	4	0.2	−0.87
4	7	1.2	2.13	5	0	0.13	5	1.2	0.13
5	4	−1.8	−0.87	5	0	0.13	3	−0.8	−1.87
6	6	0.2	1.13	7	2	2.13	3	−0.8	−1.87
7	6	0.2	1.13	4	−1	−0.87	4	0.2	−0.87
8	6	0.2	1.13	4	−1	−0.87	4	0.2	−0.87
9	5	−0.8	0.13	4	−1	−0.87	6	2.2	1.13
10	4	−1.8	−0.87	7	2	2.13	3	−0.8	−1.87
M	5.80	0	0.93	5.00	0	.13	3.80	0	−1.07

Note. The raw scores range from 1 (not at all happy) to 7 (very happy).

within-person predictors (e.g., where people are, who they are with, what they have been thinking and experiencing) should prove more fertile. In practice, most of the ICCs you find in daily life outcomes afford opportunities for both trait and state predictors.

Finding Your Centers

In regression analysis, researchers commonly *center* a predictor. The predictor variable is transformed so its mean is 0, usually by subtracting the sample's mean from each value (creating raw deviation scores) or by standardizing the variable (creating z scores). Centering predictors has two virtues. First, it makes the regression intercepts meaningful. If 0 isn't an allowable value (e.g., the outcome is on a 1–5 scale), the intercept's interpretation—the value of the outcome when the predictors are 0—is meaningless. If 0 is an interpretable value, centering the predictor nevertheless gives the intercept an intuitive meaning (the value of the outcome when the predictor is at the sample mean). Second, centering predictors avoids estimation problems and collinearity in regression models with interaction terms (Cohen et al., 2003).

In multilevel regression analysis, centering is crucial and complex (Enders & Tofighi, 2007). For ordinary multiple regression, centering is easy because there's only one center: the mean for the sample of people. But for daily life predictors that vary within people, we have two centers:

1. **Grand-mean centering.** This form uses the mean of the overall sample of scores to center each value.

2. **Person-mean centering.** Also known as *centering-within-contexts* or *group-mean centering*, this form calculates each person's individual mean and uses it to center their scores.

Using our happiness in daily life data, Table 7.2 shows what raw ratings of happiness look like when centered using grand means and person means.

Our simple, three-person data set illustrates a few key points about centering. Grand-mean centering preserves the rank order of participants. If someone is relatively happier throughout the study, for example, such as the first participant in Table 7.2, then their grand-mean–centered scores will be relatively higher. Person-mean centering, in contrast, wipes out the rank ordering of participants by eliminating between-person mean differences. Because each person is centered at his or her own mean, everyone will have a mean of 0 and a mix of positive and negative values.

Another way of saying that "grand-mean centering preserves between-person differences" is that grand-mean centering confounds between-person and within-person variance. It is hard to know what a high grand-mean–centered score means for a particular person and occasion. In Table 7.2, for example, all three participants have some occasions with a grand-mean–centered happiness score of +1.13. What does a value of 1.13 greater than the grand mean tell us? It could mean that a generally happy person is having a merely average day. For our happiest person, Person 1, 1.13 is the modal score, so it is their typical happiness. Or it could mean that a generally grumpy person is having a great day. For our least happy person, Person 3, 1.13 was their highest score. There's thus no clean, person-level interpretation of grand-mean centered scores.

Person-mean centered scores, in contrast, have an appealing interpretation for daily life research. When centered on within-person means, scores represent deviations around a person's own typical value. A score of +2, for example, means that the person reported feeling 2 points higher *relative to their own average*. Even when people have different mean levels of happiness, you know that a person-mean centered score of −1.4 means that the person had a relatively less happy day compared with his or her other days. As a result of within-person centering, the within-person regression coefficients have a within-person meaning. If a slope is 0.5, for instance, then the outcome changes by 0.5 for each unit that the predictor changes away from the person's own mean.

Although there are no absolutes, diary research follows a handful of standard centering practices. For between-person level predictors, the recommendations follow from ordinary regression modeling—it's usually sensible to grand-mean-center the predictors. An intuitive exception is when 0 is meaningful, such as whether people are in the treatment-as-usual condition (0) or the novel-treatment condition (1). For within-person level predictors, centering is different. In daily life projects, you will rarely want to grand-mean-center the scores. Such centering is common and sensible in other multilevel contexts (e.g., organizational and educational research; Enders & Tofighi, 2007), but it rarely gives you the within-person interpretation that daily life work seeks. Instead, for Level 1 variables, you will nearly always person-mean-center the predictors. This gives the scores and regression weights a more intuitive within-person interpretation. Common exceptions involve meaningful zeros, such as time points (e.g., an index of occasions ranging from 0 to k). These guidelines aren't the last word in centering, which can get subtle, but they reflect common guidance and practice for most daily life designs (Bolger & Laurenceau, 2013; Nezlek, 2012).

SOME VEXING ISSUES

When you're knee-deep in your first data set, wading through multilevel models, you'll eventually bump into three vexing issues in daily life analyses. First, how is time modeled as a predictor, if it is at all? Second, what does measurement reliability mean for daily life surveys, and how do you calculate reliability? And finally, how do you estimate statistical power and forecast sample sizes for multilevel studies, especially ones with eccentric patterns of missing data?

Understanding and Defining Time

Time lurks beneath all daily life studies. Because they intensively sample from people, daily life projects resemble longitudinal studies on a tiny time scale. The tradition that labels this method *intensive longitudinal studies* (Bolger & Laurenceau, 2013; T. A. Walls & Schafer, 2006) emphasizes that time is always an analytic issue in daily life data, even if it isn't one that interests the researchers. When planning your data analyses, then, you should consider how to represent time in your model.

In Chapter 6, we explored many ways of coding time in your data set, such as the serial order of signals, lagged orders, intervals between surveys, and durations. Coding time enables us to model it, which requires thinking about what role, if any, time plays in our planned analyses. In some cases, time is a predictor variable. A variable that captures the serial order of the occasions, for example, can be used to predict trends across the course of data collection. In other cases, time is an outcome, such as when durations are used to explore when an event happens, if it happened at all (Singer & Willett, 2003). And in others the model is time structured, such as when autocorrelated residuals or lagged predictors are included.

Including the occasion's serial order as a within-person predictor has many virtues. Consider, for example, an intensive, single-day experience sampling study in which people are asked to complete a few items about their mood and social behavior every 20 to 30 minutes. The researcher finds a significant within-person relationship between interacting with other people and positive moods. Including the "beep number," from 0 to k, allows the researcher to evaluate possible confounding third variables. Time can capture many confounds that vary within a person (Bolger & Laurenceau, 2013). People's moods and activity levels, for example, have well-established diurnal trends (Palmer, 2002; Watson, 2000), and people's daily routines structure their opportunities for social interaction, such as morning meetings, lunch breaks, and after-work happy hours. Variables like mood and social interaction can be correlated at the within-person level solely because of coincidental covariation with factors captured by the time of day.

Our impression is that time is more often included as a predictor for studies with fewer occasions, such as daily diary studies, and for studies with fixed time intervals. Time less often appears in intensive within-day experience sampling studies with random intervals and dense assessment designs, such as 6 to 10 random beeps a day for 1 or 2 weeks. As with many statistical practices, we suspect tradition is a big reason. Early experience sampling projects rarely included beep-level time predictors, and early influential introductions to analyzing daily life data didn't raise the issue.

For better or worse, time is often—if not usually—omitted in the grubby trenches of published daily life research. By omitting time, the rows of data are treated as an unordered sample of responses from someone's daily life. Although controversial, this approach is widespread in intensive, within-day experience sampling studies. An interesting conceptual justification for omitting "beep time" in experience sampling studies comes from sampling theory. Random-interval studies intend to sample from the diverse population of daily experiences. By sampling randomly with constraints (i.e., dividing the day into time bins), the design should yield a sample of occasions that represents the population of occasions, much like a stratified random sample of people from a broader group (see Chapter 2). Because the occasions were captured at different random times for each day and for each participant, researchers can credibly view a person's sample of occasions as independent elements and ignore time. This reasoning is the same philosophy implicit in cross-sectional lab research, which nearly always ignores time. College students taking part in a cross-sectional study of personality, mood, and social behavior, for example, participate on different weeks. Time of participation is almost never coded, let alone modeled, despite huge variation in the weeks (e.g., spring break and looming finals).

The natural counterargument, of course, is that choosing to interpret the rows of data as interchangeable units from a broader population of possible elements doesn't make the observations time-independent. Occasions sampled an hour apart usually resemble each other more than elements sampled days apart. Research with psychology participant pools, for example, can show time-of-semester effects (Stevens & Ash, 2001; Wang & Jentsch, 1998; Zelenski et al., 2003), so perhaps it would be wise for cross-sectional research to code and analyze time, too.

Estimating Reliability

Reliability, that evergreen test question in lower level psychology classes, is oddly absent from published daily life studies. If your cross-sectional study uses a multi-item scale—a five-item measure of subjective well-being, for example—reviewers will always ask you to report an estimate of reliability, usually a measure of internal consistency like Cronbach's alpha. But daily life studies with multi-item measures of mood and well-being rarely report evidence for reliability of the scores. Why?

The reason is that a data set with intensive, repeated assessments has more *facets* (Shavelson & Webb, 1991). In your cross-sectional well-being data, you have participants (your unit of observation) and one facet: *items*. Your data set might have 100 people who completed 5 well-being items, for 500 scores. In your daily life data, however, you have participants and two facets: items and occasions. Your data set might have 100 people who completed five items at 40 occasions, for 20,000 scores.

The challenge for estimating reliability for faceted designs is that the familiar statistics handle only one facet, not the whole design. You could estimate the item reliability via Cronbach's alpha across the five items, ignoring (unwisely) the interdependent scores and unequal participant sample sizes. You could likewise estimate the reliability of the occasions by averaging the five items at each occasion and estimating Cronbach's alpha on the total score for the 40 values. But what you want to know is the reliability of your complete assessment design—the reliability of a five-item scale completed 40 times—not merely the reliability of five-item scale or of a scale completed 40 times.

Because researchers don't encounter faceted data often, reliability in daily life data requires extending some familiar tools or learning some new ones. Exhibit 7.2 describes four ways of estimating reliability for diary data, using our example of 100 people completing a five-item scale 40 times. They each have virtues, so select the method that meshes best with your statistical knowledge and preferred software. The ICC approach is probably the best default choice for the flummoxed.

Estimation methods aside, reliability coefficients for daily life designs should be interpreted more generously. Nezlek (2017) pointed out that daily life scales, compared with cross-sectional scales, are unusually short, often just a few items. The NEO Personality Inventory-3 Extraversion subscale, for example, has 48 items (McCrae et al., 2005), but an experience sampling study of daily extraversion might have only four (Fleeson, 2001). Nezlek suggested that the cutoffs used in lab studies (e.g., $\alpha > .80$) are probably too strict for the necessarily brief scales used in daily life studies.

EXHIBIT 7.2. Four Methods for Estimating Reliability in Daily Life Data

1. Generalizability Theory

    Cronbach's alpha is ubiquitous, but alpha is a special case of Cronbach's broader *generalizability theory* of score dependability, known as "G theory" (Cronbach et al., 1972). G theory estimates the reliability of scores for nested and crossed designs, including the simple case of repeated assessments of items (Shrout & Lane, 2012). G theory isn't hard to learn (Shavelson & Webb, 1991), and Bolger and Laurenceau (2013, Chapter 7) provided a walk-through with sample code for a diary example. G theory has a lot of appeal: It yields a coefficient in the familiar alpha metric (from 0 to 1), it affords reliability estimates for a wide range of designs, and it can be estimated in software from SPSS to R (Mushquash & O'Connor, 2006; Robitzsch & Steinfeld, 2018; Vispoel et al., 2018).

2. Intraclass Correlations

    Earlier in this chapter we showed how an intraclass correlation (ICC) can represent the proportion of variance in item responses at different levels. In a daily life design, we can estimate item reliability by examining the relative variances across the levels (Bonito et al., 2012; Nezlek, 2017). In our running example, which has 100 people completing a five-item scale 40 times, you would form a three-level model: items (Level 1) nested within occasions (Level 2) nested within people (Level 3). Using the variances from an unconditional multilevel model, you can calculate a reliability coefficient functionally equivalent to Cronbach's alpha. When you know the occasion-level variance (V_2), the item-level variance (V_1), and the number of items (k), the reliability for your five-item scale across occasions would be

$$\text{Reliability} = V_2/(V_2 + [V_1/k]).$$

   The appeal of this method is that the coefficient is in the familiar alpha metric, it's easy to compute, and the quirky patterns of missingness and unequal participation in daily life data are accommodated. We encourage you to read Nezlek's (2017) and Bonito et al.'s (2012) articles for important assumptions and details.

3. Multilevel Confirmatory Factor Analysis

    If you're comfortable with confirmatory factor analysis (CFA), you probably know some reliability coefficients for CFA models (Drewes, 2000; Hancock & Mueller, 2001; Zinbarg et al., 2005). Cronbach's alpha is a special case of some of these coefficients. You can estimate reliability coefficients via a multilevel CFA (Geldhof et al., 2014). In our example, at Level 1, the five well-being items would be indicators for a latent well-being variable. The reliability of this latent variable can be estimated with the usual CFA reliability methods.

    This method is appealing for researchers who use latent-variable frameworks and software for their daily life data (e.g., Mplus or lavaan; Muthén & Muthén, 2017; Rosseel, 2012). The approach naturally handles missing data and varying observations per participant and can be extended in interesting ways for non-continuous outcomes. Coefficients like H and ω are in the same 0–1 range as α, but they are only roughly equivalent and have slightly different interpretations. We encourage reading up on multilevel CFA (Heck & Thomas, 2020), working through an example provided by Bolger and Laurenceau (2013), and learning some nitty-gritty details (Geldhof et al., 2014) if this approach appeals to you.

EXHIBIT 7.2. Four Methods for Estimating Reliability in Daily Life Data (Continued)

4. Many Facet Rasch Models

If you are familiar with Rasch and item-response models, you can apply an extension of the classic Rasch model to faceted designs. Many-facet Rasch modeling (Linacre, 1994)–known by the unpronounceable acronym MFRM–comes from educational assessment, which often has complex faceted designs (Eckes, 2011). Among its many virtues for daily life data, MFRM provides reliability coefficients for faceted designs, even for relatively sparse data with eccentric patterns of missingness.

An MFRM of daily life data would specify *items* and *occasions* as facets. The model will yield an estimated person score that is adjusted for effects of the facets along with reliability coefficients for estimated person scores (Adams, 2005; J. K. Kim & Nicewander, 1993; Linacre, 1994). FACETS software (Linacre, 2020) provides Rasch reliability, an estimate of the lower limit of the true reliability (Clauser & Linacre, 1999; Linacre, 1997); TAM, an open-source R package (Robitzsch et al., 2020), provides reliabilities for expected a posteriori (EAP) ability estimates. Curious readers can find practical overviews and tutorials for FACETS and TAM from related analytic contexts (Eckes, 2011; Lamprianou, 2020; Primi et al., 2019; Robitzsch & Steinfeld, 2018).

Planning Sample Sizes and Conducting Power Analyses

If you're planning a dissertation or a grant proposal, you will surely be asked to conduct a power analysis. Estimating power is easy for off-the-shelf regression and ANOVA models. You can conduct fancy-pants Monte Carlo simulations, apply dedicated power programs (e.g., G*Power), hunt down online calculators, or flip through printed power tables in old books (Cohen, 1969). Estimating power for daily life designs, however, is both quirky and prickly. In a cross-sectional survey, you have only one sample size: the number of participants (e.g., $n = 100$). But in a daily life study, you have at least two sample sizes: the number of participants ($n = 100$) and the number of occasions ($n = 30$). Multiplying those samples gives your expected total observations (e.g., 3,000 expected scores). So, what is your sample size: 100, 30, or 3,000? To make matters murkier, the ICC reduces your effective sample size for some analyses, so the degree of interdependence will shape the effects of sample size on power.

You can conduct multilevel power analysis with specialized software, such as Optimal Design (Raudenbush et al., 2011) or, increasingly, R packages (Bulus et al., 2019; Kleiman, 2017). Power analysis for multilevel data requires specifying the usual factors, such as your alpha level and expected effect sizes, along with some new factors. First, you'll have two sample sizes: (a) the number of clusters (people, in most daily life studies) and (b) the number of observations per cluster (occasions). Second, the ICC must be specified because power shifts as ICC values change. You can select a likely ICC value from past research; when in doubt, evaluate power for a range of ICC values (e.g., .10, .30, and .50 are sensible ones for daily life research).

The R package EMAtools (Kleiman, 2017) has useful functions for computing and displaying power curves for some multilevel models. EMAtools asks users to specify a few values: (a) the numbers of people, days, and beeps per day; and (b) the expected ICC. It displays curves for common effect sizes (e.g., $d = 0.20$, 0.50, and 0.80). Figure 7.1 depicts curves for a model with 50 people who completed six surveys per day for 7 days with an ICC of .20. Power is for a random-intercept model (e.g., the main effect of a between-person variable on the outcome). In a nod to the realities of missed surveys, the chart shows what power would be at different response rates.

Many multilevel power programs and functions can evaluate only simple hypotheses (e.g., a main effect at one level) and clean, prototypical cases (e.g., no missing data). If you wish to evaluate power for complex hypotheses or messy models, you will need to conduct Monte Carlo simulations. The simulation approach specifies parameter values for a population model, simulates a pool of data sets, and calculates the proportion of data sets in which a parameter of interest was significant (Muthén & Muthén, 2002). It's the best way to examine power for less common models, such as models with multilevel mediation, latent variables, or offbeat outcomes (e.g., ordinal, censored, and count outcomes; Long, 1997). Simulations also afford computing power to reflect messy patterns of missingness. Instead of assuming all participants have the same number of responses, for example, you can simulate realistic patterns of nonresponse (Silvia et al., 2014).

The drawback of simulating power is the need to specify values for a huge number of parameters. Simulating power for a multilevel mediation

FIGURE 7.1. Example of Power Curves to Illustrate the Influence of Effect Sizes and Within-Person Sample Sizes on Power

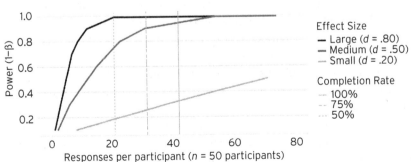

Note. This figure was generated using EMAtools (Kleiman, 2017). It is based on a design with 50 people, 7 days, six beeps per day, and an intraclass correlation of .20.

model, for example, would require specifying likely values for intercepts, slopes, and variances for many variables at several levels. A solution is to use data from prior studies as *seed data* for the simulation. Basing the simulation on real data from a similar population makes the power analysis more plausible and practical. Power simulations are easier than beginners expect, and several resources can walk you through the process (Bolger & Laurenceau, 2013, Chapter 10; Bolger et al., 2012; Muthén & Muthén, 2002).

We have no bottom-line, heuristic recommendations for sample sizes, such as the minimum number of cases you should have at each level. History shows that guidelines for minimally adequate sample sizes (e.g., clusters-to-elements rules like 30:30 or 50:20; Hox, 2002; Kreft & de Leeuw, 1998) get misinterpreted as guidelines for "sufficient power." You'll need to crunch some numbers and do a real power analysis. Nevertheless, a dominant theme in the power literature is that higher level units have a much larger effect on power than lower level units (Bickel, 2007, Chapter 10; Bolger et al., 2012; Maas & Hox, 2005). For the kinds of hypotheses that daily life researchers test, boosting power is mostly a matter of sampling more people, not more occasions. Unfortunately, adding more participants costs much more—in time, personnel, recruiting costs, and research infrastructure—than adding occasions. It can be tempting to try to make up for fewer people by expanding the occasions (e.g., adding another week of beeps to a study), but for most models the effect of occasions on power diminishes quickly. When in doubt, choose peeps over beeps.

CONCLUSION

In this chapter, we have highlighted some of the quirky and vexing issues involved with daily life data. Our goal is to prevent readers from leaping into a daily life study without first looking at the gnarled and lumpy data set they will land on. For some readers, everything in this chapter sounded familiar. If that's you, you're probably ready to go, more or less, and can easily fill some holes in your knowledge with some reading. There are many fine resources for learning multilevel modeling in general (e.g., Heck & Thomas, 2020; Robson & Pevalin, 2016) and for analyzing daily life data in particular (Bolger & Laurenceau, 2013; Nezlek, 2012; Ruwaard et al., 2018). For other readers, much of this chapter sounded foreign or forbidding. If that's you, recruit a stats collaborator, ideally during the early design stages of the project. Either way, once the data are scrubbed clean and ready to go out in public, it's time to present and publish your findings—the topic of our next chapter.

8 PRESENTING AND PUBLISHING YOUR RESEARCH

After the slog of designing, piloting, running, and monitoring your daily life study and the hours spent cleaning and analyzing your data, you may be seeing the light at the end of the tunnel—or at least the blinding glare of a projector bulb while you're presenting your slides at a conference. Sharing your research with your colleagues—through posters, presentations, and ultimately publication—is the natural endpoint of research. Your experience with presenting and publishing will serve you well when you're preparing to share your first daily life project but, like all methods, daily life methods have some methodological and statistical details that the community of researchers expects to see.

This chapter offers recommendations for researchers new to presenting and writing up daily life research. We provide tips for presenting your project and discuss the most common questions people ask during talks and poster presentations. When it's time to write, you should craft your manuscript to adhere to emerging norms for daily life articles. We distill recent guidance about article reporting standards specific to daily life research (Bolger & Laurenceau, 2013; Trull & Ebner-Priemer, 2020) and offer our own recommendations for a reader-friendly manuscript.

---

https://doi.org/10.1037/0000236-008
Researching Daily Life: A Guide to Experience Sampling and Daily Diary Methods, by P. J. Silvia and K. N. Cotter
Copyright © 2021 by the American Psychological Association. All rights reserved.

PRESENTING DAILY LIFE RESEARCH

Presenting daily life research is much like presenting other types of research. You'll still provide the audience with context for why you conducted the study; a description of your sample; and an overview of your method, findings, and implications. To prepare a daily life presentation, you should add a few core pieces of information and anticipate some common audience questions. Our guiding idea is that your audience will be unusually interested in your method. The typical conference session attracts an audience interested in the substantive topic. For a session on "New Directions in Anhedonia," for example, most attendees are there to learn about anhedonia and appetitive motivation. A conference session or poster with daily life projects, however, will attract an additional cluster of daily life researchers who are only there for the beeps. Daily life types have a lurid curiosity about how other researchers are collecting and analyzing data these days and want to see what's new. You should thus emphasize methodological details and expect questions about the nuts and bolts of your sampling and data collection process.

Making Your Presentation

When creating your presentation, try to give your audience a picture of what your study was like for the participants. When we present other types of research using widely known tasks and scales, we can cite them and be confident our audience will understand what participants did as part of the study. But because there is considerable variability among daily life studies, simply stating that you used a daily diary or experience-sampling approach won't convey the necessary texture or detail.

Your audience will want an expanded description of your method. First, provide the basic details of your procedure, such as how many days people participated in the study, how many signals were sent each day, what software or hardware was used as part of signaling or data collection, and what devices participants used. During talks, include images of the device and screenshots of sample survey items to illustrate what participants saw during the study. During poster sessions, considering bringing a lab device with a sample survey available for attendees to see or try out. The practice survey you created to train participants would be perfect (see Chapter 5).

Second, you will want to quote the items within your presentation when possible. Audience members new to daily life research may be puzzled about how a construct like paranoid ideation, marijuana craving, or daydreaming is measured in vivo, and audience members who conduct daily life research might want to borrow a few items for their next project, so show the exact wording of items and response scales. And third, your audience always wants to know about compliance and missingness, so provide descriptive statistics about the number or percentage of surveys the participants completed. "What was the response rate?" will be the first question you get if you forget to address it.

The core analyses you present will depend on your study's aims and design, of course, but one of the most valuable elements of daily life research is its wealth of descriptive information. Your audience will find basic information about variability informative, so consider including information about the variability of people's responses over the course of data collection, such as intraclass correlations (ICCs), distributions of within-person responses, and any changes over time. This information can help your audience understand the relative stability or variability of your constructs. These descriptive findings—presented as figures rather than tables, ideally—will nicely complement your primary analyses.

Finally, after creating a draft of your presentation, step back and reflect on why you chose a daily life approach. It's easy to get absorbed in our projects and assume that the rationale behind our choices is self-evident to our audience—it seems obvious to us, after all. Daily life methods are increasingly popular, but many people in your audience will be unfamiliar with this family of methods and could use some justification for why you chose this complex, technical method to study your research questions. When introducing your project, consider explicitly addressing the "Why daily life methods?" question. What new insights can a daily life approach bring to your research topic? Why is it interesting? Why couldn't you just use a lab or survey approach instead? What does it buy you? Explaining the virtues of your method will enrich your presentation and might inspire a couple people to get started in daily life work.

Common Audience Questions

Experienced presenters know that audience questions are reasonably predictable, so you can prepare for the most common kinds of queries (Feldman & Silvia, 2010; Weissman, 2013). For talks about daily life presentations, the first cluster of questions is specific to your substantive question. What do your results mean in the context of your research area?

What new questions or implications follow from it? We'll leave preparing for substantive questions in your capable rhetorical hands.

The second cluster of questions is about your daily life methodology itself. Many of these nuts-and-bolts questions will be from fellow daily life researchers, who are always eager to talk shop about the technical marginalia of the method. You should be prepared for questions on these topics from the daily life crowd:

- your exact sampling design (e.g., numbers of beeps, days, and items)
- the platform you used, how long participants had to initiate a response, whether they received automated reminders, and whether uncompleted surveys vanished
- how you tracked compliance during the study
- the overall response rate and differences between groups, if any
- if you used any special features to boost response rates (e.g., lotteries, incentives, email nudges; Chapter 5)
- how you dropped people and occasions (see Chapters 6 and 7)

Try to read the room to see if the rest of the audience cares about these technical, "inside baseball" questions. If most of the audience is there for the substantive topic, keep your responses crisp and invite the questioner to catch you afterward for the greasy nuts and bolts. People who do not conduct daily life research may ask some of these nuts-and-bolts questions, but more often you'll be asked general questions about the process of conducting daily life research. The most common topic is what the participant experience is like. Because most traditional lab and survey work involves a single data collection session, the repeated assessments of daily life research can strike researchers as intense and frazzling. Some of your audience may be interested in how participants react to this type of data collection (e.g., Do participants stay engaged? Are there issues with retention?) or what the survey experience was like for participants. Including examples of your survey in your presentation or bringing a device to demonstrate the surveys can be useful in addressing these questions. And you'll probably get questions about participant reactivity (see Chapter 3): Does taking part in the study and completing the same surveys multiple times alter people's responses to these surveys? We've found that audience members who don't conduct daily life research greatly overestimate the burden of participating and expect reactivity to be much greater than it is, so be prepared to discuss these topics (see Exhibit 8.1).

EXHIBIT 8.1. Preparing Undergraduates for Presenting

With the increasingly widespread use of daily life methods, more undergraduate students are working on daily life projects and presenting their findings at conferences. It's rare, though, for the typical research methods curriculum to cover specialized methods like experience sampling and daily diaries, so your students will probably need some extra preparation before being let loose at a conference poster session.

The first step, of course, is ensuring that students have a thorough, fluent understanding of daily life methods and the substantive research topic. We never want to put students in front of crowds of strangers until they're ready. With that foundation in place, you can focus your training on the particulars of your project. Ideally, the students were involved in running the project, such as administering research sessions, tracking compliance, setting up surveys, or cursing at the glitchy apps. If not, set up a training version of the study and have your presenters participate in the study for a few days to give them a ground-level view of how it worked and what it was like for participants. Living inside the study for a few days will make it much easier to describe the methods and handle questions about it. After this dress rehearsal, share the study's protocol documents and walk through the reasoning behind its sample, sampling design, and survey design.

Finally, work with students to practice their answers for the most likely questions. Having participated in the study will prepare students to answer most of the questions the audience will have about what the study was like for participants. Many other common questions—especially about data analysis and the finer points of the method—are technical and above the pay grade of most undergraduates. It helps to forewarn students that these questions are likely, prepare them as best you can, and reassure them that it is okay if they can't answer a question about the minutiae regarding how the signaling system schedules the quasi-random interval survey notifications. And for presentation day, a friendly face in the crowd or near the poster easel goes a long way in building confidence.

PUBLISHING DAILY LIFE RESEARCH

Just like screenplays and sonnets, scientific articles are written within tight constraints. Our manuscript must look a certain way to appeal to our audience, or at least to avoid its scorn, so much of the craft of scientific writing is understanding what your audience needs, wants, and hopes to see (Silvia, 2015). Some of writing's constraints are implicit cultural norms, like the different norms for formality and style in different areas of the sciences. Other constraints, however, are explicit rules. Journals, for example, require a certain style—American Psychological Association (APA) Style, for most of us—and set limits on words, pages, and figures to discourage garrulous and self-indulgent authors.

You already know how to navigate those constraints. If you don't, there's plenty of advice for how to craft a research manuscript (Sarnecka, 2019; Silvia, 2015, 2019; Sternberg, 2018). What readers new to daily life work need to learn are its unique article reporting standards. Psychology and its kindred fields share global reporting standards—the Journal Article Reporting Standards (JARS; Cooper, 2020)—that outline elements authors ought to include and discuss in their manuscripts. Because cross-area standards are necessarily abstract, many subfields build upon them with method-specific reporting standards, such as the CONSORT (Consolidated Standards of Reporting Trials) standards for clinical trials (Schulz et al., 2010) and the PRISMA (Preferred Reporting Items for Systematic Reviews and Meta-Analyses) guidelines for systematic reviews (Moher et al., 2009).

Daily life research hasn't evolved to the point of having formal reporting guidelines. Many researchers, however, have offered guidance that, when paired with other good practices in writing and open science, represent a great starting point. If researchers new to daily life work follow these guidelines, they won't get dinged for obvious things that experienced researchers—that is, your paper's reviewers—expect to see. Here are the main elements to include, which we've distilled from touchstone sources you ought to read (Bolger & Laurenceau, 2013; Trull & Ebner-Priemer, 2020) and our own experience as editors and reviewers (see Exhibit 8.2). The reporting elements all fall in the Method and Results sections and will entail figures, tables, and possibly supplemental material.

What Goes in the Method Section?

Article reporting guidelines will have the biggest effect on your Method section. Here are key points to discuss.

Participants

Who took part? Aside from the usual information about recruitment and sampling, you should note if the daily life method itself screened out participants or caused them to decline to participate. For example, a project might require that participants own a particular kind of smartphone. A few participants might get dropped for tech calamities that effectively precluded providing data. Some privacy-conscious participants will decline to take part in studies that require them to install an app on their device or record images and sound during their day. As with all studies, you should justify your sample size. We're sympathetic to calls for including a priori power analyses, but because of the complexity of multilevel power analysis (see Chapter 7) we suspect that they won't be common until journals require them.

Sampling and Survey Designs

What were your sampling and survey designs (Chapters 2 and 3), and why did you choose them? Here you explain your design for the number of days,

EXHIBIT 8.2. Essential Information for a Daily Life Research Article

A daily life research article will look a little different than a typical lab-based article. Here are some key points to hit in your Method and Results sections.

Method Section

- **Participants.** Explain how you selected your sample and your sample size and note whether the daily life methods affected participants' eligibility, exclusion, or willingness to consent to take part.
- **Sampling and survey design.** Explain your sampling design and your choice of days, beeps, and items. Include a summary of your measures and the daily life survey, with response options and directions. To aid reviewers and other daily life researchers, include the full survey as a table, appendix, or online supplemental file.
- **Data collection system and devices.** Describe what devices people used outside the lab (yours or theirs) and the gritty details of your data collection system (e.g., how signals worked, how surveys were accessed, how time was stamped, and whether missed surveys vanished).
- **In-lab procedures.** What did people do in person in the lab? This would include any surveys and tasks as well as any instructions about the daily life portion of the study, practice survey completion, and device training.
- **Out-of-lab procedures.** Detail the specifics of signaling (i.e., when and how often people were signaled), any ongoing contact with participants (e.g., check-ins), incentives to encourage engagement, and methods for checking in and nudging.

Results Section

- **Exclusions.** If any individual surveys or participants were excluded from analyses, explain your criteria and note how many surveys or people were excluded for each reason.
- **Response rates.** Describe the response rates for the daily life surveys, including the total number and range of completed surveys, the average response rate, and, if applicable, the response rates for subgroups of interest.
- **Descriptive statistics and correlations.** In the text, summarize the descriptive statistics at both the within-person and between-person levels. Provide full descriptive information and correlations among all daily life variables within tables or figures.
- **Intraclass correlation coefficients.** Intraclass correlations are a staple of daily life research articles. Provide a short summary of these values for your constructs and, if you have a lot, include them in a table or figure.
- **Modeling and estimation details.** Specify how the variables were modeled, such as their levels, any transformations, and centering. Include whether effects were fixed or random and how time was modeled, if at all. The specific model estimator, software package, and version should be noted.

beeps, and items. Did you use event-based sampling? If so, later in the Method section be sure to describe how you defined the event to the participants and specify whether the event-based surveys were always available or whether there were limits (e.g., completing surveys about conflict only when at work, not at home). Did you sample using fixed or random intervals? If so, describe how many signals—in total and per day—were sent to participants. For fixed-interval studies, include the exact signal times. For random-interval studies, discuss the parameters that guided your random signals, such as the range of the day people could expect signals, whether people could select a time window for signals (e.g., 8:00 a.m.–8:00 p.m. vs. noon–midnight), and any constraints on randomization (e.g., chopping the day into time bins).

Surveys

You probably have many measures—lab tasks, personality surveys, or interviews—in addition to your daily life survey. We recommend different subheadings for different assessment modes to frame the daily life measurement. For your daily life items, include the full survey in a table, appendix, or online supplemental file. The survey should clearly indicate response options, scale anchors, and any branching or skipping. We've found that some reviewers and editors suggest removing the survey in the interests of page space. You can either move the survey to a site for online supplemental material (e.g., Open Science Framework; https://www.osf.io) or point out that modern reporting guidelines recommend including it.

Signal and Survey Systems

Describe the system used for signaling and surveying (see Chapter 4). How did you signal participants? What was the signal like? Did it make a sound, flash a visual notification on a screen, or vibrate? What happened when people didn't respond to the signal? Did people get reminders, perhaps after 30 or 60 seconds? Depending on your signaling system, there may be other relevant details, such as the ability of the participants to mute or alter the appearance of signals. Next, describe the data collection process. Was this the same system used for signaling, or was it separate? How did people access the surveys within the data collection system? Could people save their progress and complete the survey later? Could people access missed surveys? If you are using paper surveys, you should also describe how many survey forms people were given and how they returned their completed responses. For electronic collection systems, you could include a figure with an example of the appearance of the surveys. As an aside, many digital systems, from dusty Palm Pilots to modern apps, allow you to export the code file that defines the survey's look and behavior. Placing the code in an online supplemental file would save time for other researchers and foster replicability.

Devices

If relevant, describe what software and devices were used to send signals and give surveys. In some cases, participants will be given lab-owned devices to use during the study. For any lab devices used, you should provide information regarding the operating system, any restrictions placed upon the devices (e.g., all apps besides those used by the study were disabled), and other device specifications, such as screen size. In other cases, participants may be using their own devices to complete the study. Because there will be greater heterogeneity in these devices than in lab devices, you should provide the basic requirements for the devices, such as compatible operating systems, software versions, or other requirements needed by your study (e.g., able to receive texts, has an integrated GPS). In instances when both participant and lab devices are used, you should indicate how many people used personal and lab devices. If the device is more uncommon or offbeat than a smartphone or tablet—such as accelerometers, dosimeters, and cardiac monitors—you should note the manufacturer and full device name.

Participant Training

How did you explain the study to the participants and teach them how to interact with the signals and surveys (Chapter 5)? Include how terms and items were defined for participants—a crucial point for event-based designs—and describe any instructions provided about the surveys, guidance for using the technology, ways to get in touch if issues arose, and any practice surveys they completed. When including the details, make sure you indicate what participants were instructed to do if signaled during times when they are unavailable to complete surveys (e.g., at work, when driving) and how missing surveys could impact their future participation or compensation. Consider including your full session script as online supplemental material.

Monitoring and Nudging

How did you monitor data collection and nudge response rates higher? If you included planned check-ins with participants (Chapter 5), provide the details. Did you contact people via email, phone call, or text? If you met in person, was it at your lab or elsewhere? Was everyone contacted at specific points during the study (e.g., on Day 4), or did you selectively contact participants (e.g., anyone with fewer than 20% of surveys completed after 3 days)? If you selectively contacted only some participants, note the percentage of participants who got extra nudging.

Incentives

Explain any incentives you used to boost participant engagement. For example, perhaps you had cash payments that escalated when people met response rate thresholds, lotteries held for people who completed at least 70% of the surveys, or extra payments when both members of a dyad completed 80% of the surveys. Reporting the percentage of participants who attained the incentive will help other researchers plan for how many carrots to buy.

What Goes in the Results Section?

Your Results section won't require as much expansion as your Method section. Although daily life studies vary in many ways, there are some common statistical reporting practices that should find their way into your Results section.

Excluded Occasions and People

Results sections usually begin with a section of greasy nuts and bolts (Salovey, 2000). Here you should include information about any people or surveys that were excluded. Evaluating the quality of your data is complex, and there's no consensus on excluding people and occasions (Chapter 6), so clearly describe and justify whatever method you used to determine which people or beeps to exclude from analyses. In addition, note how many surveys were excluded and how many people were excluded entirely. If you are using multiple criteria for exclusion, such as inattentive behavior during a lab session or completing too few daily life surveys, you should specify how many people were excluded for each criterion.

Response Rates

Alongside exclusion information, describe the response rates for your study. Include the total number of surveys completed, the average number of surveys completed per person, and the range of surveys completed per person. Additional statistics (e.g., measures of variability) and metrics (e.g., the percentage of people who completed at least 50% or 70% of the surveys) is helpful. Depending on the study, you may also choose to report response rates broken down by groups, conditions, or demographic characteristics.

For example, a clinical trial would report response rates for each group and discuss if they're notably different.

Descriptive Statistics

Next up is providing readers with descriptive information about your variables. It's always a good idea to include a table with descriptive statistics for all your variables, but part of the appeal of daily life research is its rich descriptive data. You should, at minimum, summarize your descriptive findings, even if description is not the primary aim of your project. Full descriptive information and correlations between all daily life variables should also be included within a table. Because your data are nested, you can describe your daily life variables at both the within-person and between-person levels. Report a reliability coefficient if it is relevant (see Chapter 7).

Intraclass Correlations

When providing descriptive statistics, don't forget your ICCs. The percentage of variance at each level is inherently interesting to daily life researchers, who are curious about within-person variability. Knowing the ICC also sets the stage for your statistical model and helps future researchers who need plausible ICC values for a power analysis. If you have only a couple ICCs, you can mention them in the text; if you have a lot, consider creating a figure or adding them to a table.

Modeling

Most daily life projects use some flavor of multilevel modeling, but whatever you do, lay out the modeling details. For the typical project, you should specify your predictors and outcomes, identify their model level, and specify any data recoding or transformations. Your centering decisions should be clearly stated, and any categorical or limited outcomes (e.g., counts, durations, or censored variables) should be highlighted (Long, 1997). Be sure to note whether effects are modeled as fixed or random. Time can play many roles in analyzing daily life data (Chapter 6), including being omitted, so describe how time is included, if at all, in your model.

Estimation

The differences between estimation methods are notable enough that you should explicitly note your estimator, such as simple maximum likelihood (ML), restricted ML, ML with robust standard errors, or Bayesian methods. Likewise, the differences between software packages—and versions of the same package—are large enough that you should be explicit about your software and version.

Open Science Opportunities

Throughout, we've mentioned some reporting guidelines that broadly fall under the umbrella of open science practices (Nosek et al., 2015). We recommend creating a public archive for your project's materials, such as an Open Science Framework project, so other researchers can build on your hard work. Many journals allow and host online supplemental material, but we prefer to place the materials in an archive that we can manage. This allows us to expand the archive as new scripts, data, and materials become available, to link past and future archives, and to ensure that the materials are publicly available.

Ideal elements for a public project archive are the full daily life survey, the app code for the survey (if relevant), materials used for participant training, and syntax and code for cleaning, wrangling, and analyzing your data. We recommend sharing your preprint, such as via PsyArXiv (https://www.psyarxiv.com), so that your work can reach your audience sooner. Many of the references in this book, for example, we first read as preprints. And if you preregistered your project—an emerging topic for daily life work (Kirtley et al., 2020)—the project archive will have your entire research life cycle, from planning to publication, in one spot.

Sharing the project's data files is ideal. Given the diversity of ethical and legal frameworks that guide research data in different countries, however, as well as quickly evolving guidance on data sharing from governments and funding agencies, we recommend consulting your institution's research office and your funder for guidance about posting the data. Keep in mind that many modern survey systems collect extensive data on people's internet provider (IP) addresses, GPS locations, and device details, so concerns about possible reidentification from raw data are serious (Ross et al., 2018).

CONCLUSION

The final stages of a research project—sharing your findings through presentations and publications—are rewarding but daunting tasks. We hope that the recommendations and tips provided in this chapter alleviate some of the anxiety of sharing your daily life work for the first time. And once you've wrapped up your first daily life project and found it a good peer-reviewed home, you have probably been bitten by the in vivo bug and are itching to start the process all over again. We wish you good luck: May all your response rates be high and your notifications be audible.

References

Adams, R. J. (2005). Reliability as a measurement design effect. *Studies in Educational Evaluation, 31*(2–3), 162–172. https://doi.org/10.1016/j.stueduc.2005.05.008

Armey, M. F., Crowther, J. H., & Miller, I. W. (2011). Changes in ecological momentary assessment reported affect associated with episodes of non-suicidal self-injury. *Behavior Therapy, 42*(4), 579–588. https://doi.org/10.1016/j.beth.2011.01.002

Barta, W. D., Tennen, H., & Litt, M. D. (2012). Measurement reactivity in diary research. In M. R. Mehl & T. S. Conner (Eds.), *Handbook of research methods for studying daily life* (pp. 108–123). Guilford Press.

Baumeister, R. F., Wright, B. R. E., & Carreon, D. (2019). Self-control "in the wild": Experience sampling study of trait and state self-regulation. *Self and Identity, 18*(5), 494–528. https://doi.org/10.1080/15298868.2018.1478324

Bellamy, N., Sothern, R. B., & Campbell, J. (2004). Aspects of diurnal rhythmicity in pain, stiffness, and fatigue in patients with fibromyalgia. *The Journal of Rheumatology, 31*(2), 379–389.

Benedek, M., Jauk, E., Kerschenbauer, K., Anderwald, R., & Grond, L. (2017). Creating art: An experience sampling study in the domain of moving image art. *Psychology of Aesthetics, Creativity, and the Arts, 11*(3), 325–334. https://doi.org/10.1037/aca0000102

Berenson, K. R. (2018). *Managing your research data and documentation*. American Psychological Association. https://doi.org/10.1037/0000068-000

Berkman, E. T., Giuliani, N. R., & Pruitt, A. K. (2014). Comparison of text messaging and paper-and-pencil for ecological momentary assessment of food craving and intake. *Appetite, 81*, 131–137. https://doi.org/10.1016/j.appet.2014.06.010

Bertz, J. W., Epstein, D. H., Reamer, D., Kowalczyk, W. J., Phillips, K. A., Kennedy, A. P., Jobes, M. L., Ward, G., Plitnick, B. A., Figueiro, M. G., Rea, M. S., & Preston, K. L. (2019). Sleep reductions associated with illicit opioid use and clinic-hour changes during opioid agonist treatment for opioid dependence: Measurement by electronic diary and actigraphy. *Journal of Substance Abuse Treatment, 106,* 43–57. https://doi.org/10.1016/j.jsat.2019.08.011

Bickel, R. (2007). *Multilevel analysis for applied research: It's just regression!* Guilford Press.

Black, A. C., Harel, O., & Matthews, G. (2012). Techniques for analyzing intensive longitudinal data with missing values. In M. R. Mehl & T. S. Conner (Eds.), *Handbook of research methods for studying daily life* (pp. 339–356). Guilford Press.

Bolger, N., & Laurenceau, J. P. (2013). *Intensive longitudinal methods: An introduction to diary and experience sampling research.* Guilford Press.

Bolger, N., Stadler, G., & Laurenceau, J. P. (2012). Power analysis for intensive longitudinal studies. In M. R. Mehl & T. S. Conner (Eds.), *Handbook of research methods for studying daily life* (pp. 285–301). Guilford Press.

Bollich, K. L., Doris, J. M., Vazire, S., Raison, C. L., Jackson, J. J., & Mehl, M. R. (2016). Eavesdropping on character: Assessing everyday moral behaviors. *Journal of Research in Personality, 61,* 15–21. https://doi.org/10.1016/j.jrp.2015.12.003

Bonito, J. A., Ruppel, E. K., & Keyton, J. (2012). Reliability estimates for multilevel designs in group research. *Small Group Research, 43*(4), 443–467. https://doi.org/10.1177/1046496412437614

Bouwmans, M. E. J., Bos, E. H., Hoenders, H. J. R., Oldehinkel, A. J., & de Jonge, P. (2017). Sleep quality predicts positive and negative affect but not vice versa: An electronic diary study in depressed and healthy individuals. *Journal of Affective Disorders, 207,* 260–267. https://doi.org/10.1016/j.jad.2016.09.046

Brennan, R. L. (2001). *Generalizability theory.* Springer. https://doi.org/10.1007/978-1-4757-3456-0

Brown, N. A., Blake, A. B., & Sherman, R. A. (2017). A snapshot of the life as lived: Wearable cameras in social and personality psychological science. *Social Psychological & Personality Science, 8*(5), 592–600. https://doi.org/10.1177/1948550617703170

Bulus, M., Dong, N., Kelcey, B., & Spybrook, J. (2019). *PowerUpR: Power analysis tools for multilevel randomized experiments* (Version 1.0.4) [Computer software]. https://CRAN.R-project.org/package=PowerUpR

Burgin, C. J., Silvia, P. J., Eddington, K. M., & Kwapil, T. R. (2012). Palm or cell? Comparing personal digital assistants and cell phones for experience sampling research. *Social Science Computer Review, 31*(2), 244–251. https://doi.org/10.1177/0894439312441577

Carlson, E. B., Field, N. P., Ruzek, J. I., Bryant, R. A., Dalenberg, C. J., Keane, T. M., & Spain, D. A. (2016). Advantages and psychometric validation of proximal intensive assessments of patient-reported outcomes collected in daily life. *Quality of Life Research, 25*(3), 507–516. https://doi.org/10.1007/s11136-015-1170-9

Carter, B. L., Day, S. X., Cinciripini, P. M., & Wetter, D. W. (2007). Momentary health interventions: Where are we and where are we going? In A. A. Stone, S. Shiffman, A. A. Atienza, & L. Nebeling (Eds.), *The science of real-time data capture: Self-reports in health research* (pp. 289–307). Oxford University Press.

Cattell, R. B. (1966). The data box: Its ordering of total resources in terms of possible relations systems. In R. B. Cattell (Ed.), *Handbook of multivariate experimental psychology* (pp. 67–128). Rand McNally.

Christensen, A. P. (2020). Openness to experience. In V. P. Glăveanu (Ed.), *The Palgrave encyclopedia of the possible*. Springer. https://doi.org/10.1007/978-3-319-98390-5_113-1

Clauser, B., & Linacre, J. M. (1999). Relating Cronbach and Rasch reliabilities. *Rasch Measurement Transactions, 13*(2), 696.

Cohen, J. (1969). *Statistical power analysis for the behavioral sciences*. Academic Press.

Cohen, J., Cohen, P., West, S. G., & Aiken, L. S. (2003). *Applied multiple regression/correlation analysis for the behavioral sciences* (3rd ed.). Erlbaum.

Collins, R. P., Litman, J. A., & Spielberger, C. D. (2004). The measurement of perceptual curiosity. *Personality and Individual Differences, 36*(5), 1127–1141. https://doi.org/10.1016/S0191-8869(03)00205-8

Conner, T. S., Brookie, K. L., Richardson, A. C., & Polak, M. A. (2015). On carrots and curiosity: Eating fruit and vegetables is associated with greater flourishing in daily life. *British Journal of Health Psychology, 20*(2), 413–427. https://doi.org/10.1111/bjhp.12113

Conner, T. S., & Lehman, B. J. (2012). Getting started: Launching a study in daily life. In M. R. Mehl & T. S. Conner (Eds.), *Handbook of research methods for studying daily life* (pp. 89–107). Guilford Press.

Conner, T. S., & Reid, K. A. (2012). Effects of intensive mobile happiness reporting in daily life. *Social Psychological & Personality Science, 3*(3), 315–323. https://doi.org/10.1177/1948550611419677

Conner, T. S., Tennen, H., Fleeson, W., & Barrett, L. F. (2009). Experience sampling methods: A modern idiographic approach to personality research. *Social and Personality Psychology Compass, 3*(3), 292–313. https://doi.org/10.1111/j.1751-9004.2009.00170.x

Cooper, H. (2020). *Reporting quantitative research in psychology: How to meet APA style journal article reporting standards* (2nd ed.). American Psychological Association. https://doi.org/10.1037/0000178-000

Cotter, K. N. (2020). *Mental control of musical imagery: Combining behavioral and experience-sampling approaches* [Doctoral dissertation, University of North Carolina at Greensboro]. NC DOCKS. http://libres.uncg.edu/ir/uncg/f/Cotter_uncg_0154D_12953.pdf

Cotter, K. N., Christensen, A. P., & Silvia, P. J. (2019). Understanding inner music: A dimensional approach to musical imagery. *Psychology of Aesthetics, Creativity, and the Arts, 13*(4), 489–503. https://doi.org/10.1037/aca0000195

Cotter, K. N., & Silvia, P. J. (2017). Measuring mental music: Comparing retrospective and experience sampling methods for assessing musical imagery. *Psychology of Aesthetics, Creativity, and the Arts, 11*(3), 335–343. https://doi.org/10.1037/aca0000124

Cotter, K. N., & Silvia, P. J. (2019). Ecological assessment in research on aesthetics, creativity and the arts: Basic concepts, common questions, and gentle warnings. *Psychology of Aesthetics, Creativity, and the Arts, 13*(2), 211–217. https://doi.org/10.1037/aca0000218

Cotter, K. N., & Silvia, P. J. (2020). Tuning the inner radio: The mental control of musical imagery in everyday environments. *Psychology of Music, 48*(6), 876–878. https://doi.org/10.1177/0305735618824987

Cronbach, L. J., Gleser, G. C., Nanda, H., & Rajaratnam, N. (1972). *The dependability of behavioral measurements: Theory of generalizability for scores and profiles*. Wiley.

Csikszentmihalyi, M. (1975). *Beyond boredom and anxiety: The experience of play in work and games*. Jossey-Bass.

Cybulski, G. (2011). *Ambulatory impedance cardiography: The systems and their applications*. Springer. https://doi.org/10.1007/978-3-642-11987-3

Denissen, J. J. A., Butalid, L., Penke, L., & van Aken, M. A. G. (2008). The effects of weather on daily mood: A multilevel approach. *Emotion, 8*(5), 662–667. https://doi.org/10.1037/a0013497

DeVellis, R. F. (2017). *Scale development: Theory and applications* (4th ed.). SAGE.

De Vuyst, H. J., Dejonckheere, E., Van der Gucht, K., & Kuppens, P. (2019). Does repeatedly reporting positive or negative emotions in daily life have an impact on the level of emotional experiences and depressive symptoms over time? *PLoS ONE, 14*(6), e0219121. https://doi.org/10.1371/journal.pone.0219121

DeYoung, C. G., Quilty, L. C., & Peterson, J. B. (2007). Between facets and domains: 10 aspects of the Big Five. *Journal of Personality and Social Psychology, 93*(5), 880–896. https://doi.org/10.1037/0022-3514.93.5.880

Dodds, W. B., Monroe, K. B., & Grewal, D. (1991). Effects of price, brand, and store information on buyers' product evaluations. *Journal of Marketing Research, 28*(3), 307–319.

Drewes, D. W. (2000). Beyond the Spearman–Brown: A structural approach to maximal reliability. *Psychological Methods, 5*(2), 214–227. https://doi.org/10.1037/1082-989X.5.2.214

Eaton, L. G., & Funder, D. C. (2001). Emotional experience in daily life: Valence, variability, and rate of change. *Emotion, 1*(4), 413–421. https://doi.org/10.1037/1528-3542.1.4.413

Ebner-Priemer, U. W., Eid, M., Kleindienst, N., Stabenow, S., & Trull, T. J. (2009). Analytic strategies for understanding affective (in)stability and other dynamic processes in psychopathology. *Journal of Abnormal Psychology, 118*(1), 195–202. https://doi.org/10.1037/a0014868

Eckes, T. (2011). *Introduction to many-facet Rasch measurement: Analyzing and evaluating rater-mediated assessments*. Peter Lang. https://doi.org/10.3726/978-3-653-04844-5

Eddington, K. M., Burgin, C. J., Silvia, P. J., Fallah, N., Majestic, C., & Kwapil, T. R. (2017). The effects of psychotherapy for major depressive disorder on daily mood and functioning: A longitudinal experience sampling study. *Cognitive Therapy and Research, 41*(2), 266–277. https://doi.org/10.1007/s10608-016-9816-7

Eddington, K. M., & Foxworth, T. E. (2012). Dysphoria and self-focused attention: Effects of failure feedback on task performance and goal setting. *Journal of Social and Clinical Psychology, 31*(9), 933–951. https://doi.org/10.1521/jscp.2012.31.9.933

Eddington, K. M., Silvia, P. J., Foxworth, T. E., Hoet, A., & Kwapil, T. R. (2015). Motivational deficits differentially predict improvement in a randomized trial of self-system therapy for depression. *Journal of Consulting and Clinical Psychology, 83*(3), 602–616. https://doi.org/10.1037/a0039058

Eisele, G., Vachon, H., Lafit, G., Kuppens, P., Houben, M., Myin-Germeys, I., & Viechtbauer, W. (2020). The effects of sampling frequency and questionnaire length on perceived burden, compliance, and careless responding in experience sampling data in a student population. *Assessment*. https://doi.org/10.1177/1073191120957102

Enders, C. K. (2010). *Applied missing data analysis*. Guilford Press.

Enders, C. K., & Tofighi, D. (2007). Centering predictor variables in cross-sectional multilevel models: A new look at an old issue. *Psychological Methods, 12*(2), 121–138. https://doi.org/10.1037/1082-989X.12.2.121

Feldman, D. B., & Silvia, P. J. (2010). *Public speaking for psychologists: A light-hearted guide to research presentations, job talks, and other opportunities to embarrass yourself*. American Psychological Association.

Fleeson, W. (2001). Toward a structure- and process-integrated view of personality: Traits as density distribution of states. *Journal of Personality and Social Psychology, 80*(6), 1011–1027. https://doi.org/10.1037/0022-3514.80.6.1011

Fleeson, W. (2004). Moving personality beyond the person–situation debate: The challenge and the opportunity of within-person variability. *Current Directions in Psychological Science, 13*(2), 83–87. https://doi.org/10.1111/j.0963-7214.2004.00280.x

Garrison, K. A., Pal, P., O'Malley, S. S., Pittman, B. P., Gueorguieva, R., Rojiani, R., Scheinost, D., Dallery, J., & Brewer, J. A. (2020). Craving to quit: A randomized controlled trial of smartphone app-based mindfulness training for smoking cessation. *Nicotine & Tobacco Research, 22*(3), 324–331. https://doi.org/10.1093/ntr/nty126

Geldhof, G. J., Preacher, K. J., & Zyphur, M. J. (2014). Reliability estimation in a multilevel confirmatory factor analysis framework. *Psychological Methods, 19*(1), 72–91. https://doi.org/10.1037/a0032138

George, M. J., Rivenbark, J. G., Russell, M. A., Ng'eno, L., Hoyle, R. H., & Odgers, C. L. (2019). Evaluating the use of commercially available wearable wristbands to capture adolescents' daily sleep duration. *Journal of Research on Adolescence, 29*(3), 613–626. https://doi.org/10.1111/jora.12467

Granholm, E., Holden, J. L., Mikhael, T., Link, P. C., Swendsen, J., Depp, C., Moore, R. C., & Harvey, P. D. (2020). What do people with schizophrenia do all day? Ecological momentary assessment of real-world functioning in schizophrenia. *Schizophrenia Bulletin, 46*(2), 242–251. https://doi.org/10.1093/schbul/sbz070

Green, A. S., Rafaeli, E., Bolger, N., Shrout, P. E., & Reis, H. T. (2006). Paper or plastic? Data equivalence in paper and electronic diaries. *Psychological Methods, 11*(1), 87–105. https://doi.org/10.1037/1082-989X.11.1.87

Gunthert, K. C., & Wenze, S. J. (2012). Daily diary methods. In M. R. Mehl & T. S. Conner (Eds.), *Handbook of research methods for studying daily life* (pp. 144–159). Guilford Press.

Hamaker, E. L. (2012). Why researchers should think "within-person": A paradigmatic rationale. In M. R. Mehl & T. S. Conner (Eds.), *Handbook of research methods for studying daily life* (pp. 43–61). Guilford Press.

Hamilton, N. A., Affleck, G., Tennen, H., Karlson, C., Luxton, D., Preacher, K. J., & Templin, J. L. (2008). Fibromyalgia: The role of sleep in affect and in negative event reactivity and recovery. *Health Psychology, 27*(4), 490–497. https://doi.org/10.1037/0278-6133.27.4.490

Hancock, G. R., & Mueller, R. O. (2001). Rethinking construct reliability within latent variable systems. In R. Cudeck, S. du Toit, & D. Sörbom (Eds.), *Structural equation modeling: Present and future* (pp. 195–216). Scientific Software International.

Harari, G. M., Lane, N. D., Wang, R., Crosier, B. S., Campbell, A. T., & Gosling, S. D. (2016). Using smartphones to collect behavioral data in psychological science: Opportunities, practical considerations, and challenges. *Perspectives on Psychological Science, 11*(6), 838–854. https://doi.org/10.1177/1745691616650285

Harper, K. L., Eddington, K. M., & Silvia, P. J. (2020). Perfectionism and loneliness: The role of expectations and social hopelessness in daily life. *Journal of Social and Clinical Psychology, 39*(2), 117–139. https://doi.org/10.1521/jscp.2020.39.02.117

Heck, R. H., & Thomas, S. L. (2020). *An introduction to multilevel modeling techniques: MLM and SEM approaches using Mplus* (4th ed.). Routledge. https://doi.org/10.4324/9780429060274

Hektner, J. M., Schmidt, J. A., & Csikszentmihalyi, M. (2007). *Experience sampling method: Measuring the quality of everyday life*. SAGE.

Henry, G. T. (1990). *Practical sampling*. SAGE. https://doi.org/10.4135/9781412985451

Henson, R. K. (2001). Understanding internal consistency reliability estimates: A conceptual primer on coefficient alpha. *Measurement & Evaluation in*

Counseling & Development, 34(3), 177–189. https://doi.org/10.1080/07481756.2002.12069034

Himmelstein, P. H., Woods, W. C., & Wright, A. G. C. (2019). A comparison of signal- and event-contingent ambulatory assessment of interpersonal behavior and affect in social situations. *Psychological Assessment, 31*(7), 952–960. https://doi.org/10.1037/pas0000718

Hoet, A. C., Burgin, C. J., Eddington, K. M., & Silvia, P. J. (2018). Reports of therapy skill use and their efficacy in daily life in the short-term treatment of depression. *Cognitive Therapy and Research, 42*(2), 184–192. https://doi.org/10.1007/s10608-017-9852-y

Hopper, J. W., Su, Z., Looby, A. R., Ryan, E. T., Penetar, D. M., Palmer, C. M., & Lukas, S. E. (2006). Incidence and patterns of polydrug use and craving for ecstasy in regular ecstasy users: An ecological momentary assessment study. *Drug and Alcohol Dependence, 85*(3), 221–235. https://doi.org/10.1016/j.drugalcdep.2006.04.012

Houtveen, J. H., & de Geus, E. J. C. (2009). Noninvasive psychophysiological ambulatory recordings: Study design and data analysis strategies. *European Psychologist, 14*(2), 132–141. https://doi.org/10.1027/1016-9040.14.2.132

Howard, D., Klettke, B., Ling, M., Krug, I., & Fuller-Tyskiewicz, M. (2019). Does body dissatisfaction influence sexting behaviors in daily life? *Computers in Human Behavior, 101*, 320–326. https://doi.org/10.1016/j.chb.2019.07.033

Hox, J. (2002). *Multilevel analysis: Techniques and applications.* Erlbaum. https://doi.org/10.4324/9781410604118

Hoyle, R. H., Stephenson, M. T., Palmgreen, P., Lorch, E. P., & Donohew, R. L. (2002). Reliability and validity of a brief measure of sensation seeking. *Personality and Individual Differences, 32*(3), 401–414. https://doi.org/10.1016/S0191-8869(01)00032-0

Intille, S., Haynes, C., Maniar, D., Ponnada, A., & Manjourides, J. (2016, September). µEMA: Microinteraction-based ecological momentary assessment (EMA) using a smartwatch [Conference session]. In *Proceedings of the ACM International Conference on Ubiquitous Computing* (pp. 1124–1128). https://doi.org/10.1145/2971648.2971717

Jacobson, N. C. (2020, January 15–17). *Compliance thresholds in intensive longitudinal data: Worse than listwise deletion: Call for action* [Paper presentation]. Society for Ambulatory Assessment conference, Melbourne, Australia. https://www.nicholasjacobson.com/files/talks/SAA2020_Compliance_Thresholds.pdf

Jacobson, N. C., Chow, S. M., & Newman, M. G. (2019). The differential time-varying effect model (DTVEM): A tool for diagnosing and modeling time lags in intensive longitudinal data. *Behavior Research Methods, 51*(1), 295–315. https://doi.org/10.3758/s13428-018-1101-0

Jahng, S., Wood, P. K., & Trull, T. J. (2008). Analysis of affective instability in ecological momentary assessment: Indices using successive difference and group comparison via multilevel modeling. *Psychological Methods, 13*(4), 354–375. https://doi.org/10.1037/a0014173

Ji, L., Chow, S. M., Schermerhorn, A. C., Jacobson, N. C., & Cummings, E. M. (2018). Handling missing data in the modeling of intensive longitudinal data. *Structural Equation Modeling, 25*(5), 715–736. https://doi.org/10.1080/10705511.2017.1417046

Jones, A., Remmerswaal, D., Verveer, I., Robinson, E., Franken, I. H. A., Wen, C. K. F., & Field, M. (2019). Compliance with ecological momentary assessment protocols in substance users: A meta-analysis. *Addiction, 114*(4), 609–619. https://doi.org/10.1111/add.14503

Kamarck, T. W., Shiffman, S. M., Smithline, L., Goodie, J. L., Thompson, H. S., Ituarte, P. H. G., Jong, J. Y.-K., Pro, V., Paty, J. A., Kassel, J. D., Gnys, M., & Perz, W. (1998). The Diary of Ambulatory Behavioral States: A new approach to the assessment of psychosocial influences on ambulatory cardiovascular activity. In D. S. Krantz & A. Baum (Eds.), *Technology and methods in behavioral medicine* (pp. 163–193). Erlbaum.

Kane, M. J., Brown, L. H., McVay, J. C., Silvia, P. J., Myin-Germeys, I., & Kwapil, T. R. (2007). For whom the mind wanders, and when: An experience-sampling study of working memory and executive control in daily life. *Psychological Science, 18*(7), 614–621. https://doi.org/10.1111/j.1467-9280.2007.01948.x

Kane, M. J., Gross, G. M., Chun, C. A., Smeekens, B. A., Meier, M. E., Silvia, P. J., & Kwapil, T. R. (2017). For whom the mind wanders, and when, varies across laboratory and daily-life settings. *Psychological Science, 28*(9), 1271–1289. https://doi.org/10.1177/0956797617706086

Karwowski, M., Lebuda, I., Szumski, G., & Firkowska-Mankiewicz, A. (2017). From moment-to-moment to day-to-day: Experience sampling and diary investigations in adults' everyday creativity. *Psychology of Aesthetics, Creativity, and the Arts, 11*(3), 309–324. https://doi.org/10.1037/aca0000127

Kashdan, T. B., Gallagher, M. W., Silvia, P. J., Winterstein, B. P., Breen, W. E., Terhar, D., & Steger, M. F. (2009). The Curiosity and Exploration Inventory–II: Development, factor structure, and psychometrics. *Journal of Research in Personality, 43*(6), 987–998. https://doi.org/10.1016/j.jrp.2009.04.011

Kashdan, T. B., & Steger, M. F. (2007). Curiosity and pathways to well-being and meaning in life: Traits, states, and everyday behaviors. *Motivation and Emotion, 31*(3), 159–173. https://doi.org/10.1007/s11031-007-9068-7

Kim, J. K., & Nicewander, W. A. (1993). Ability estimation for conventional tests. *Psychometrika, 58*(4), 587–599. https://doi.org/10.1007/BF02294829

Kim, Y., Dykema, J., Stevenson, J., Black, P., & Moberg, D. P. (2019). Straightlining: Overview of measurement, comparison of indicators, and effects in mail–web mixed-mode surveys. *Social Science Computer Review, 37*(2), 214–233. https://doi.org/10.1177/0894439317752406

Kirtley, O. J., Lafit, G., Achterhof, R., Hiekkaranta, A. P., & Myin-Germeys, I. (2020). Making the black box transparent: A template and tutorial for (pre-)registration of studies using experience sampling methods (ESM). *PsyArXiv*. Advance online publication. https://doi.org/10.31234/osf.io/seyq7

Kleiman, E. (2017). *EMAtools: Data management tools for real-time monitoring/ecological momentary assessment data* (Version 0.1.3) [Computer software]. https://CRAN.R-project.org/package=EMAtools

Korotitsch, W. J., & Nelson-Gray, R. O. (1999). An overview of self-monitoring research in assessment and treatment. *Psychological Assessment, 11*(4), 415–425. https://doi.org/10.1037/1040-3590.11.4.415

Kreft, I., & de Leeuw, J. (1998). *Introducing multilevel modeling*. SAGE.

Kuntsche, E., & Cooper, M. L. (2010). Drinking to have fun and to get drunk: Motives as predictors of weekend drinking over and above usual drinking habits. *Drug and Alcohol Dependence, 110*(3), 259–262. https://doi.org/10.1016/j.drugalcdep.2010.02.021

Kwapil, T. R., Silvia, P. J., Myin-Germeys, I., Anderson, A. J., Coates, S. A., & Brown, L. H. (2009). The social world of the socially anhedonic: Exploring the daily ecology of asociality. *Journal of Research in Personality, 43*(1), 103–106. https://doi.org/10.1016/j.jrp.2008.10.008

Lamprianou, I. (2020). *Applying the Rasch model in social sciences using R and BlueSky statistics*. Routledge.

Landes, D. S. (2000). *Revolution in time: Clocks and the making of the modern world* (2nd ed.). Belknap Press.

Lane, S. J., Heddle, N. M., Arnold, E., & Walker, I. (2006). A review of randomized controlled trials comparing the effectiveness of hand held computers with paper methods for data collection. *BMC Medical Informatics and Decision Making, 6*(1), 23. https://doi.org/10.1186/1472-6947-6-23

Larsen, R. J., & Kasimatis, M. (1990). Individual differences in entrainment of mood to the weekly calendar. *Journal of Personality and Social Psychology, 58*(1), 164–171. https://doi.org/10.1037/0022-3514.58.1.164

Laughland, A., & Kvavilashvili, L. (2018). Should participants be left to their own devices? Comparing paper and smartphone diaries in psychological research. *Journal of Applied Research in Memory and Cognition, 7*(4), 552–563. https://doi.org/10.1016/j.jarmac.2018.09.002

Law, M. K., Fleeson, W., Arnold, E. M., & Furr, R. M. (2016). Using negative emotions to trace the experience of borderline personality pathology: Interconnected relationships revealed in an experience sampling study. *Journal of Personality Disorders, 30*(1), 52–70. https://doi.org/10.1521/pedi_2015_29_180

Le, B., Choi, H. N., & Beal, D. J. (2006). Pocket-sized psychology studies: Exploring daily diary software for Palm Pilots. *Behavior Research Methods, 38*(2), 325–332. https://doi.org/10.3758/BF03192784

Lee, K., & Ashton, M. C. (2018). Psychometric properties of the HEXACO–100. *Assessment, 25*(5), 543–556. https://doi.org/10.1177/1073191116659134

Lehman, B. J., Cane, A. C., Tallon, S. J., & Smith, S. F. (2015). Physiological and emotional responses to subjective social evaluative threat in daily life. *Anxiety, Stress, and Coping, 28*(3), 321–339. https://doi.org/10.1080/10615806.2014.968563

Linacre, J. M. (1994). *Many-facet Rasch measurement*. Mesa Press.

Linacre, J. M. (1997). KR–20 or Rasch reliability: Which tells the "truth"? *Rasch Measurement Transactions, 11*, 580–581. https://www.rasch.org/rmt/rmt131.htm

Linacre, J. M. (2020). *FACETS computer program for many-facet Rasch measurement* (Version 3.83.3) [Computer software]. https://www.winsteps.com/facets.htm

Lipton, R. B., Buse, D. C., Hall, C. B., Tennen, H., Defreitas, T. A., Borkowski, T. M., Grosberg, B. M., & Haut, S. R. (2014). Reduction in perceived stress as a migraine trigger: Testing the "let-down headache" hypothesis. *Neurology, 82*(16), 1395–1401. https://doi.org/10.1212/WNL.0000000000000332

Little, R. J. A., & Rubin, D. B. (1987). *Statistical analysis with missing data*. Wiley.

Little, T. D. (2013). *Longitudinal structural equation modeling*. Guilford Press.

Liu, Y., & West, S. G. (2016). Weekly cycles in daily report data: An overlooked issue. *Journal of Personality, 84*(5), 560–579. https://doi.org/10.1111/jopy.12182

Long, J. S. (1997). *Regression models for categorical and limited dependent variables*. SAGE.

Maas, C. J. M., & Hox, J. J. (2005). Sufficient sample sizes for multilevel modeling. *Methodology, 1*(3), 86–92. https://doi.org/10.1027/1614-2241.1.3.86

Mackesy-Amiti, M. E., & Boodram, B. (2018). Feasibility of ecological momentary assessment to study mood and risk behavior among young people who inject drugs. *Drug and Alcohol Dependence, 187*, 227–235. https://doi.org/10.1016/j.drugalcdep.2018.03.016

Maniaci, M. R., & Rogge, R. D. (2014). Caring about carelessness: Participant inattention and its effects on research. *Journal of Research in Personality, 48*, 61–83. https://doi.org/10.1016/j.jrp.2013.09.008

Manuoğlu, E., & Uysal, A. (2020). Motivation for different Facebook activities and well-being: A daily experience sampling study. *Psychology of Popular Media Culture, 9*(4), 456–464. https://doi.org/10.1037/ppm0000262

McCabe, K. O., Mack, L., & Fleeson, W. (2012). A guide for data cleaning in experience sampling studies. In M. R. Mehl & T. S. Conner (Eds.), *Handbook of research methods for studying daily life* (pp. 321–338). Guilford Press.

McCrae, R. R., Costa, P. T., Jr., & Martin, T. A. (2005). The NEO–PI–3: A more readable revised NEO Personality Inventory. *Journal of Personality Assessment, 84*(3), 261–270. https://doi.org/10.1207/s15327752jpa8403_05

McDevitt-Murphy, M. E., Luciano, M. T., & Zakarian, R. J. (2018). Use of ecological momentary assessment and intervention in treatment with adults. *Focus, 16*(4), 370–375. https://doi.org/10.1176/appi.focus.20180017

McKibben, W. B., & Silvia, P. J. (2016). Inattentive and socially desirable responding: Addressing subtle threats to validity in quantitative counseling research. *Counseling Outcome Research and Evaluation, 7*(1), 53–64. https://doi.org/10.1177/2150137815613135

McKnight, P. E., McKnight, K. M., Sidani, S., & Figueredo, A. J. (2007). *Missing data: A gentle introduction*. Guilford Press.

McLean, D. C., Nakamura, J., & Csikszentmihalyi, M. (2017). Explaining system missing: Missing data and experience sampling method. *Social Psychological and Personality Science*, *8*(4), 434–441. https://doi.org/10.1177/1948550617708015

McNeish, D. (2018). Thanks coefficient alpha, we'll take it from here. *Psychological Methods*, *23*(3), 412–433. https://doi.org/10.1037/met0000144

Mehl, M. R., & Conner, T. S. (Eds.). (2012). *Handbook of research methods for studying daily life*. Guilford Press.

Mehl, M. R., & Robbins, M. L. (2012). Naturalistic observation sampling: The Electronically Activated Recorder (EAR). In M. R. Mehl & T. S. Conner (Eds.), *Handbook of research methods for studying daily life* (pp. 176–192). Guilford Press.

Miller, G. (2012). The smartphone psychology manifesto. *Perspectives on Psychological Science*, *7*(3), 221–237. https://doi.org/10.1177/1745691612441215

Moher, D., Liberati, A., Tetzlaff, J., Altman, D. G., & the PRISMA Group. (2009). Preferred Reporting Items for Systematic Reviews and Meta-Analyses: The PRISMA statement. *PLoS Medicine*, *6*(7), e1000097. https://doi.org/10.1371/journal.pmed.1000097

Moskowitz, D. S., & Sadikaj, G. (2012). Event-contingent recording. In M. R. Mehl & T. S. Conner (Eds.), *Handbook of research methods for studying daily life* (pp. 160–175). Guilford Press.

Muraven, M., Collins, R. L., Morsheimer, E. T., Shiffman, S., & Paty, J. A. (2005). The morning after: Limit violations and the self-regulation of alcohol consumption. *Psychology of Addictive Behaviors*, *19*(3), 253–262. https://doi.org/10.1037/0893-164X.19.3.253

Muraven, M., Collins, R. L., Shiffman, S., & Paty, J. A. (2005). Daily fluctuations in self-control demands and alcohol intake. *Psychology of Addictive Behaviors*, *19*(2), 140–147. https://doi.org/10.1037/0893-164X.19.2.140

Mushquash, C., & O'Connor, B. P. (2006). SPSS and SAS programs for generalizability theory analyses. *Behavior Research Methods*, *38*(3), 542–547. https://doi.org/10.3758/BF03192810

Muthén, L. K., & Muthén, B. O. (2002). How to use a Monte Carlo study to decide on sample size and determine power. *Structural Equation Modeling*, *9*(4), 599–620. https://doi.org/10.1207/S15328007SEM0904_8

Muthén, L. K., & Muthén, B. O. (2017). *Mplus user's guide* (8th ed.).

Naylor, F. D. (1981). A state–trait curiosity inventory. *Australian Psychologist*, *16*(2), 172–183. https://doi.org/10.1080/00050068108255893

Nezlek, J. B. (2012). *Diary methods for social and personality psychology*. SAGE. https://doi.org/10.4135/9781446287903

Nezlek, J. B. (2017). A practical guide to understanding reliability in studies of within-person variability. *Journal of Research in Personality*, *69*, 149–155. https://doi.org/10.1016/j.jrp.2016.06.020

Nosek, B. A., Alter, G., Banks, G. C., Borsboom, D., Bowman, S. D., Breckler, S. J., Buck, S., Chambers, C. D., Chin, G., Christensen, G., Contestabile, M., Dafoe, A., Eich, E., Freese, J., Glennerster, R., Goroff, D., Green, D. P., Hesse, B., Humphreys, M., . . . Yarkoni, T. (2015). Promoting an open research culture. *Science*, *348*(6242), 1422–1425. https://doi.org/10.1126/science.aab2374

Nusbaum, E. C., Silvia, P. J., Beaty, R. E., Burgin, C. J., Hodges, D., & Kwapil, T. R. (2014). Listening between the notes: Aesthetic chills in everyday music listening. *Psychology of Aesthetics, Creativity, and the Arts*, *8*, 104–109. https://doi.org/10.1037/a0034867

Oleynick, V. C., DeYoung, C. G., Hyde, E., Kaufman, S. B., Beaty, R. E., & Silvia, P. J. (2017). Openness/Intellect: The core of the creative personality. In G. J. Feist, R. Reiter-Palmon, & J. C. Kaufman (Eds.), *Cambridge handbook of creativity and personality research* (pp. 9–27). Cambridge University Press. https://doi.org/10.1017/9781316228036.002

Olson, R., Carney, A. K., & Patrick, J. H. (2019). Associations between gratitude and spirituality: An experience sampling approach. *Psychology of Religion and Spirituality*, *11*(4), 449–452. https://doi.org/10.1037/rel0000164

Ono, M., Schneider, S., Junghaenel, D. U., & Stone, A. A. (2019). What affects the completion of ecological momentary assessments in chronic pain research? An individual patient data meta-analysis. *Journal of Medical Internet Research*, *21*(2), e11398. https://doi.org/10.2196/11398

Palmer, J. D. (2002). *The living clock: The orchestrator of biological rhythms*. Oxford University Press.

Papp, L. M., Cummings, E. M., & Goeke-Morey, M. C. (2009). For richer, for poorer: Money as a topic of marital conflict in the home. *Family Relations*, *58*(1), 91–103. https://doi.org/10.1111/j.1741-3729.2008.00537.x

Peeters, F., Berkhof, J., Delespaul, P., Rottenberg, J., & Nicolson, N. A. (2006). Diurnal mood variation in major depressive disorder. *Emotion*, *6*(3), 383–391. https://doi.org/10.1037/1528-3542.6.3.383

Phillips, M. M., Phillips, K. T., Lalonde, T. L., & Dykema, K. R. (2014). Feasibility of text messaging for ecological momentary assessment of marijuana use in college students. *Psychological Assessment*, *26*(3), 947–957. https://doi.org/10.1037/a0036612

Primi, R., Silvia, P. J., Jauk, E., & Benedek, M. (2019). Applying many-facet Rasch modeling in the assessment of creativity. *Psychology of Aesthetics, Creativity, and the Arts*, *13*(2), 176–186. https://doi.org/10.1037/aca0000230

Ratcliff, R. (1993). Methods for dealing with reaction time outliers. *Psychological Bulletin*, *114*(3), 510–532. https://doi.org/10.1037/0033-2909.114.3.510

Rathbun, S. L., Song, X., Neustifter, B., & Shiffman, S. (2013). Survival analysis with time varying covariates measured at random times by design. *Journal of the Royal Statistical Society Series C: Applied Statistics*, *62*(3), 419–434. https://doi.org/10.1111/j.1467-9876.2012.01064.x

Raudenbush, S. W., Spybrook, J., Congdon, R., Liu, X. F., Martinez, A., Bloom, H., & Hill, C. (2011). *Optimal design software for multilevel and longitudinal research* (Version 3.01) [Computer software]. https://sites.google.com/site/optimaldesignsoftware

Reis, H. T. (2012). Why researchers should think "real-world": A conceptual rationale. In M. R. Mehl & T. S. Conner (Eds.), *Handbook of research methods for studying daily life* (pp. 3–21). Guilford Press.

Reis, H. T., & Gable, S. L. (2000). Event sampling and other methods for studying daily experience. In H. T. Reis & C. M. Judd (Eds.), *Handbook of research methods in social and personality psychology* (pp. 190–222). Cambridge University Press.

Reis, H. T., Sheldon, K. M., Gable, S. L., Roscoe, J., & Ryan, R. M. (2000). Daily well-being: The role of autonomy, competence, and relatedness. *Personality and Social Psychology Bulletin, 26*(4), 419–435. https://doi.org/10.1177/0146167200266002

Rintala, A., Wampers, M., Myin-Germeys, I., & Viechtbauer, W. (2019). Response compliance and predictors thereof in studies using the experience sampling method. *Psychological Assessment, 31*(2), 226–235. https://doi.org/10.1037/pas0000662

Robbins, M. L., & Kubiak, T. (2014). Ecological momentary assessment in behavioral medicine: Research and practice. In D. I. Motofsky (Ed.), *Handbook of behavioral medicine* (Vol. 1, pp. 429–446). Wiley. https://doi.org/10.1002/9781118453940.ch20

Robitzsch, A., Kiefer, T., & Wu, M. (2020). *TAM: Test analysis modules* (Version 3.5.19) [Computer software]. https://CRAN.R-project.org/package=TAM

Robitzsch, A., & Steinfeld, J. (2018). Item response models for human ratings: Overview, estimation methods, and implementation in R. *Psychological Test and Assessment Modeling, 60*(1), 101–139.

Robson, K., & Pevalin, D. (2016). *Multilevel modeling in plain language.* SAGE.

Ross, M. W., Iguchi, M. Y., & Panicker, S. (2018). Ethical aspects of data sharing and research participant protections. *American Psychologist, 73*(2), 138–145. https://doi.org/10.1037/amp0000240

Rosseel, Y. (2012). lavaan: An R package for structural equation modeling. *Journal of Statistical Software, 48*(2), 1–36. https://doi.org/10.18637/jss.v048.i02

Ruwaard, J., Kooistra, L., & Thong, M. (2018). *Ecological momentary assessment in mental health research: A practical introduction, with examples in R.* APH Mental Health. https://jruwaard.github.io/aph_ema_handbook/

Ryan, R. M., Bernstein, J. H., & Brown, K. W. (2010). Weekends, work, and well-being: Psychological need satisfactions and day of the week effects on mood, vitality, and physical symptoms. *Journal of Social and Clinical Psychology, 29*(1), 95–122. https://doi.org/10.1521/jscp.2010.29.1.95

Salovey, P. (2000). Results that get results: Telling a good story. In R. J. Sternberg (Ed.), *Guide to publishing in psychology journals* (pp. 121–132). Cambridge University Press. https://doi.org/10.1017/CBO9780511807862.009

Santangelo, P. S., Koenig, J., Funke, V., Parzer, P., Resch, F., Ebner-Priemer, U. W., & Kaess, M. (2017). Ecological momentary assessment of affective and interpersonal instability in adolescent non-suicidal self-injury. *Journal of Abnormal Child Psychology*, *45*(7), 1429–1438. https://doi.org/10.1007/s10802-016-0249-2

Sarnecka, B. W. (2019). *The writing workshop: Write more, write better, be happier in academia*. Author.

Schimmack, U. (2003). Affect measurement in experience sampling research. *Journal of Happiness Studies*, *4*(1), 79–106. https://doi.org/10.1023/A:1023661322862

Schneider, S., Choi, S. W., Junghaenel, D. U., Schwartz, J. E., & Stone, A. A. (2013). Psychometric characteristics of daily diaries for the Patient-Reported Outcomes Measurement Information System (PROMIS®): A preliminary investigation. *Quality of Life Research*, *22*(7), 1859–1869. https://doi.org/10.1007/s11136-012-0323-3

Schneider, S., & Stone, A. A. (2016). Ambulatory and diary methods can facilitate the measurement of patient-reported outcomes. *Quality of Life Research*, *25*(3), 497–506. https://doi.org/10.1007/s11136-015-1054-z

Schooler, J. W. (2002). Re-representing consciousness: Dissociations between experience and meta-consciousness. *Trends in Cognitive Sciences*, *6*(8), 339–344. https://doi.org/10.1016/S1364-6613(02)01949-6

Schulz, K. F., Altman, D. G., & Moher, D. (2010). CONSORT 2010 statement: Updated guidelines for reporting parallel group randomised trials. *British Medical Journal*, *23*. https://doi.org/10.1136/bmj.c332

Schwartz, N. (2012). Why researchers should think "real-time": A cognitive rationale. In M. R. Mehl & T. S. Conner (Eds.), *Handbook of research methods for studying daily life* (pp. 22–42). Guilford Press.

Shavelson, R. J., & Webb, N. M. (1991). *Generalizability theory: A primer*. SAGE.

Sheldon, K. M., Ryan, R., & Reis, H. T. (1996). What makes for a good day? Competence and autonomy in the day and in the person. *Personality and Social Psychology Bulletin*, *22*(12), 1270–1279. https://doi.org/10.1177/01461672962212007

Shiffman, S. (2007). Designing protocols for ecological momentary assessment. In A. A. Stone, S. Shiffman, A. A. Atienza, & L. Nebeling (Eds.), *The science of real-time data capture: Self-reports in health research* (pp. 27–53). Oxford University Press.

Shiffman, S. (2009). How many cigarettes did you smoke? Assessing cigarette consumption by global report, time-line follow-back, and ecological momentary assessment. *Health Psychology*, *28*(5), 519–526. https://doi.org/10.1037/a0015197

Shrout, P. E., & Lane, S. P. (2012). Psychometrics. In M. R. Mehl & T. S. Conner (Eds.), *Handbook of research methods for studying daily life* (pp. 302–320). Guilford Press.

Shrout, P. E., Stadler, G., Lane, S. P., McClure, M. J., Jackson, G. L., Clavél, F. D., Iida, M., Gleason, M. E. J., Xu, J. H., & Bolger, N. (2018). Initial elevation bias in subjective reports. *Proceedings of the National Academy of Sciences of the United States of America, 115*(1), E15–E23. https://doi.org/10.1073/pnas.1712277115

Silvia, P. J. (2015). *Write it up: Practical strategies for writing and publishing journal articles*. American Psychological Association. https://doi.org/10.1037/14470-000

Silvia, P. J. (2019). *How to write a lot: A practical guide to productive academic writing* (2nd ed.). American Psychological Association. https://doi.org/10.1037/0000109-000

Silvia, P. J. (2020). *Select a sample*. SAGE.

Silvia, P. J., & Kashdan, T. B. (2017). Curiosity and interest: The benefits of thriving on novelty and challenge. In C. R. Snyder, S. J. Lopez, L. M. Edwards, & S. C. Marques (Eds.), *The Oxford handbook of positive psychology* (3rd ed.). Oxford University Press. Advance online publication. https://doi.org/10.1093/oxfordhb/9780199396511.013.29

Silvia, P. J., Kwapil, T. R., Eddington, K. M., & Brown, L. H. (2013). Missed beeps and missing data: Dispositional and situational predictors of non-response in experience sampling research. *Social Science Computer Review, 31*(4), 471–481. https://doi.org/10.1177/0894439313479902

Silvia, P. J., Kwapil, T. R., Walsh, M. A., & Myin-Germeys, I. (2014). Planned missing-data designs in experience-sampling research: Monte Carlo simulations of efficient designs for assessing within-person constructs. *Behavior Research Methods, 46*(1), 41–54. https://doi.org/10.3758/s13428-013-0353-y

Singer, J. D., & Willett, J. B. (2003). *Applied longitudinal data analysis: Modeling change and event occurrence*. Oxford University Press. https://doi.org/10.1093/acprof:oso/9780195152968.001.0001

Smart Richman, L., Pek, J., Pascoe, E., & Bauer, D. J. (2010). The effects of perceived discrimination on ambulatory blood pressure and affective responses to interpersonal stress modeled over 24 hours. *Health Psychology, 29*(4), 403–411. https://doi.org/10.1037/a0019045

Smith, J. K. (2014). *The museum effect: How museums, libraries, and cultural institutions educate and civilize society*. Rowman & Littlefield.

Soffer-Dudek, N., & Shahar, G. (2011). Daily stress interacts with trait dissociation to predict sleep-related experiences in young adults. *Journal of Abnormal Psychology, 120*(3), 719–729. https://doi.org/10.1037/a0022941

Sperry, S. H., Kwapil, T. R., Eddington, K. M., & Silvia, P. J. (2018). Psychopathology, everyday behaviors, and autonomic activity in daily life: An ambulatory impedance cardiography study of depression, anxiety, and hypomanic traits. *International Journal of Psychophysiology, 129*, 67–75. https://doi.org/10.1016/j.ijpsycho.2018.04.008

Srinivas, P., Bodke, K., Ofner, S., Keith, N. R., Tu, W., & Clark, D. O. (2019). Context-sensitive ecological momentary assessment: Application of user-centered design for improving user satisfaction and engagement during self-report. *JMIR mHealth and uHealth*, *7*(4), e10894. https://doi.org/10.2196/10894

Stein, K. F., & Corte, C. M. (2003). Ecologic momentary assessment of eating-disordered behaviors. *International Journal of Eating Disorders*, *34*(3), 349–360. https://doi.org/10.1002/eat.10194

Sternberg, R. J. (Ed.). (2018). *Guide to publishing in psychology journals* (2nd ed.). Cambridge University Press. https://doi.org/10.1017/CBO9780511807862

Stevens, C. D., & Ash, R. A. (2001). The conscientiousness of students in subject pools: Implications for "laboratory" research. *Journal of Research in Personality*, *35*(1), 91–97. https://doi.org/10.1006/jrpe.2000.2310

Stone, A. A., Bachrach, C. A., Jobe, J. B., Kurtzman, H. S., & Cain, V. S. (Eds.). (1999). *The science of self-report: Implications for research and practice*. Psychology Press. https://doi.org/10.4324/9781410601261

Stone, A. A., Broderick, J. E., Schwartz, J. E., Shiffman, S., Litcher-Kelly, L., & Calvanese, P. (2003). Intensive momentary reporting of pain with an electronic diary: Reactivity, compliance, and patient satisfaction. *Pain*, *104*(1–2), 343–351. https://doi.org/10.1016/S0304-3959(03)00040-X

Stone, A. A., Shiffman, S., Atienza, A. A., & Nebeling, L. (2007). Historical roots and rationale of ecological momentary assessment (EMA). In A. A. Stone, S. Shiffman, A. A. Atienza, & L. Nebeling (Eds.), *The science of real-time data capture: Self-reports in health research* (pp. 3–10). Oxford University Press.

Stone, A. A., Shiffman, S., Schwartz, J. E., Broderick, J. E., & Hufford, M. R. (2002). Patient non-compliance with paper diaries. *British Medical Journal*, *324*(7347), 1193–1194. https://doi.org/10.1136/bmj.324.7347.1193

Strunk, W., Jr., & White, E. B. (2000). *The elements of style* (4th ed.). Longman.

Tennen, H., Affleck, G., Coyne, J. C., Larsen, R. J., & Delongis, A. (2006). Paper and plastic in daily diary research: Comment on Green, Rafaeli, Bolger, Shrout, and Reis (2006). *Psychological Methods*, *11*(1), 112–118. https://doi.org/10.1037/1082-989X.11.1.112

Tourangeau, R., Rips, L. J., & Rasinski, K. (2000). *The psychology of survey response*. Cambridge University Press. https://doi.org/10.1017/CBO9780511819322

Trull, T. J., & Ebner-Priemer, U. (2013). Ambulatory assessment. *Annual Review of Clinical Psychology*, *9*, 151–176. https://doi.org/10.1146/annurev-clinpsy-050212-185510

Trull, T. J., & Ebner-Priemer, U. W. (2020). Ambulatory assessment in psychopathology research: A review of recommended reporting guidelines and current practices. *Journal of Abnormal Psychology*, *129*(1), 56–63. https://doi.org/10.1037/abn0000473

Tyler, K. A., & Olson, K. (2018). Examining the feasibility of ecological momentary assessment using short message service surveying with homeless youth:

Lessons learned. *Field Methods, 30*(2), 91–104. https://doi.org/10.1177/1525822X18762111

Vachon, H., Bourbousson, M., Deschamps, T., Doron, J., Bulteau, S., Sauvaget, A., & Thomas-Ollivier, V. (2016). Repeated self-evaluations may involve familiarization: An exploratory study related to ecological momentary assessment designs in patients with major depressive disorder. *Psychiatry Research, 245,* 99–104. https://doi.org/10.1016/j.psychres.2016.08.034

Vispoel, W. P., Morris, C. A., & Kilinc, M. (2018). Applications of generalizability theory and their relations to classical test theory and structural equation modeling. *Psychological Methods, 23*(1), 1–26. https://doi.org/10.1037/met0000107

Walls, F. L., & Gagnepain, J. J. (1992). Environmental sensitivities of quartz oscillators. *IEEE Transactions on Ultrasonics, Ferroelectrics, and Frequency Control, 39*(2), 241–249. https://doi.org/10.1109/58.139120

Walls, T. A., & Schafer, J. L. (Eds.). (2006). *Models for intensive longitudinal data.* Oxford University Press. https://doi.org/10.1093/acprof:oso/9780195173444.001.0001

Wang, A. Y., & Jentsch, F. G. (1998). Point-of-time effects across the semester: Is there a sampling bias? *The Journal of Psychology: Interdisciplinary and Applied, 132*(2), 211–219. https://doi.org/10.1080/00223989809599160

Washnik, N. J., Phillips, S. L., & Teglas, S. (2016). Student's music exposure: Full-day personal dose measurements. *Noise & Health, 18*(81), 98–103. https://doi.org/10.4103/1463-1741.178510

Watson, D. (2000). *Mood and temperament.* Guilford Press.

Webb, E. J., Campbell, D. T., Schwartz, R. D., & Sechrest, L. (1966). *Unobtrusive measures: Nonreactive research in the social sciences.* Rand McNally.

Weissman, J. (2013). *In the line of fire: How to handle tough questions . . . When it counts* (2nd ed.). Pearson/FT Press.

Wheeler, L., & Nezlek, J. (1977). Sex differences in social participation. *Journal of Personality and Social Psychology, 35*(10), 742–754. https://doi.org/10.1037/0022-3514.35.10.742

Wheeler, L., & Reis, H. T. (1991). Self-recording of everyday life events: Origins, types, and uses. *Journal of Personality, 59*(3), 339–354. https://doi.org/10.1111/j.1467-6494.1991.tb00252.x

Wilt, J., & Revelle, W. (2009). Extraversion. In M. R. Leary & R. H. Hoyle (Eds.), *Handbook of individual differences in social behavior* (pp. 27–45). Guilford Press.

Wray, T. B., Kahler, C. W., & Monti, P. M. (2016). Using ecological momentary assessment (EMA) to study sex events among very high-risk men who have sex with men (MSM). *AIDS and Behavior, 20*(10), 2231–2242. https://doi.org/10.1007/s10461-015-1272-y

Wray, T. B., Merrill, J. E., & Monti, P. M. (2014). Using ecological momentary assessment (EMA) to assess situation-level predictors of alcohol use and alcohol-related consequences. *Alcohol Research: Current Reviews, 36*(1), 19–27.

Xu, X., Tupy, S., Robertson, S., Miller, A. L., Correll, D., Tivis, R., & Nigg, C. R. (2018). Successful adherence and retention to daily monitoring of physical activity: Lessons learned. *PLoS One*, *13*(9), e0199838. https://doi.org/10.1371/journal.pone.0199838

Yang, Y. S., Ryu, G. W., & Choi, M. (2019). Factors associated with daily completion rates in a smartphone-based ecological momentary assessment study. *Healthcare Informatics Research*, *25*(4), 332–337. https://doi.org/10.4258/hir.2019.25.4.332

Zelenski, J. M., Rusting, C. L., & Larsen, R. J. (2003). Consistency in the time of experiment participation and personality correlates: A methodological note. *Personality and Individual Differences*, *34*(4), 547–558. https://doi.org/10.1016/S0191-8869(01)00218-5

Zhang, C., & Conrad, F. G. (2014). Speeding in web surveys: The tendency to answer very fast and its association with straightlining. *Survey Research Methods*, *8*(2), 127–155. https://doi.org/10.18148/srm/2014.v8i2.5453

Zhou, Z. E., Meier, L. L., & Spector, P. E. (2019). The spillover effects of coworker, supervisor, and outsider workplace incivility on work-to-family conflict: A weekly diary design. *Journal of Organizational Behavior*, *40*(9–10), 1000–1012. https://doi.org/10.1002/job.2401

Zinbarg, R. E., Revelle, W., Yovel, I., & Li, W. (2005). Cronbach's α, Revelle's β, and McDonald's ωH: Their relations with each other and two alternative conceptualizations of reliability. *Psychometrika*, *70*(1), 123–133. https://doi.org/10.1007/s11336-003-0974-7

Index

A

Accessibility, 64
Active sampling strategies, passive vs., 32
Additional variables, 101
Ambulatory assessment, as term, 5
American Psychological Association (APA) Style, 131
Analytic data file, 99–102
Analyzing data, 111–125
   centering a predictor, 117–118
   estimating reliability, 121–123
   nested and nonindependent observations, 113–117
   planning sample size and conducting power analyses, 123–125
   understanding and defining time, 119–120
   with unequal participation, 112–113
ANOVA models, 123
APA (American Psychological Association) Style, 131
Apps
   collecting surveys through, 56
   contingency plans when using, 75
   monitoring participant use in, 87–88
   preparation for use of, 72
   training research teams for, 73, 82
Assessing data quality, 102–109
   excluding participants, 106–109
   identification of screen-outs, 104–106
   missing data, 102–104
Audience questions, in presentations, 129–130

B

Barta, W. D., 49
Beeper studies, 5. *See also* Daily life methods
Beeps
   excluding, 104–105
   missing by, 104
   omitting time of, 120
   on self-report surveys, 36–38
   signaling participants through, 55
Best practices, for self-report surveys, 37
Between-person level
   of daily diaries, 114
   daily life methods used to assess, 14
Biases, recall, 9, 26–27
"Blue Monday," 95
Bolger, N., 109, 122
Branching, 46–47, 71
Broad sampling, 18
Buzzes, signaling participants through, 55

C

Calendar days, 95–96
Careless responses, 105
Cattell, R. B., 103
Centering a predictor, 117–118
CFA (confirmatory factor analysis), 122
Change, motivation for, 50
Check-ins during the study, 88–89, 91
Cleaning up data files, 95–96
Clock time, 43
Coding time, 119
Collecting data, 69–92
   common methods of, 56
   describing methods for, in research article, 133

157

158 • Index

improving response rates and data quality, 89–91
preparation. *See* Preparation for study
remotely, 84
running the study, 83–89
sending signals vs., 54–55
Compensation, 73
Compliance rate, calculating, 37
Compression, in daily life surveys, 35
Conditional branching, 46–47
Confirmatory factor analysis (CFA), 122
Confirming responses, 42
Conflicts, common participant questions about, 73
Conner, T. S., 4, 22
Consolidated Standards of Reporting Trials (CONSORT), 132
CONSORT (Consolidated Standards of Reporting Trials), 132
Consumer psychology, 77
Contingency plans, 74–75
Continuous sampling, 32
Correlation analysis
  describing, in research article, 133
  and unequal participation, 112–113
Costs, 63–65
Cronbach's alpha, 121–122
Cross-level interactions, daily life methods used to assess, 15
Curiosity, scales for measuring, 41

D

Daily diaries, 24–27
  in experience sampling studies, 32
  levels of, 114
  long vs. wide format of data from, 98
  and missed surveys, 62
  random intervals for, 27
  signaling participants for, 54
Daily life methods, 3–15
  common labels for, 5
  defining features of, 4, 5–11
  experimental methods vs., 12
  intensive assessment over time for, 10–11
  longitudinal methods vs., 13
  natural environments for, 6–7
  real-time data collection for, 8–10
  research questions for, 14–15
  survey methods vs., 12–13
  as term, 4

Data, 93–109
  analyzing. *See* Analyzing data
  assessing quality of, 102–109
  cleaning up, 95–96
  collecting your. *See* Collecting data
  common issues with, 119–125
  compiling your, 78–79
  evaluating pilot, 76–78
  merging, 99–102
  missing, 102–103
  organizing your. *See* Organizing data
  peculiar qualities of data, 112–118
  privacy of, 65–67
  restructuring, 96–99
  screening out, 104–109
  sharing project, 138
  taking stock of, 94
Data quality
  assessing, 102–109
  improving, 89–91
  intensive assessment to estimate, 10
  and speeding up a survey, 41
Data security, 65–67
Days, self-report survey, 36
Descriptive statistics, 102, 133, 137
Devices
  costs of, 63–64
  for data collection, 55, 57–58
  describing, in methods section, 135
  possible issues with, 75
  preparation for use of, 72
Diaries, daily. *See* Daily diaries
Diary research, 5, 118. *See also* Daily diaries
Digital clocks, 61
Discrete events, event-based sampling for, 20–21
Duplicate matches, 101
Durations, 96
Duration to complete, 39

E

Ecological momentary assessment (EMA), 5
Ecological momentary interventions, 12
Electronic data collection
  contingency plans for, 75–76
  and electronic system identifiers, 100
  response rates with, 91
  time stamping in, 105
Electronic system identifiers, 100
EMA (ecological momentary assessment), 5

Email, signaling participants through, 55
EMAtools, 124
End-of-day design, 24–25, 100
Equipment, 55–58
Errors, in time stamping, 61
ESM (experience sampling methods), 5
Estimating reliability, 121–123
Ethics, 65–66, 138
Evaluating pilot data files, 76–78
Event-based sampling
    about, 19–22
    in experience sampling studies, 32
    missed surveys in, 86
    as passive sampling, 32
    research article describing, 134
    and salience, 90
    signaling participants in, 55
    unequal participation in, 113
Event time, 43
Exclusions
    determining criteria for, 106–107
    in research article, 133, 136
Experience sampling, 28, 46. *See also* Random-interval sampling
Experience sampling methods (ESM), 5
Experimental methods, daily life methods vs., 12
Extraversion, 39

F

Faceted designs, 121
FACETS software, 123
Fairly frequent events, event-based sampling for, 21
FAQ sheet, for research teams, 82
Feedback, and reactivity, 50
Field test. *See* Piloting your study
Fixed-interval sampling
    about, 22–27
    documenting time in, 96
    as passive sampling, 32
    random vs., 29
    research article describing, 134
Fleeson, W., 40
Frequency
    daily life methods used to assess, 14
    and frequency tables, 102
    intensive assessment to estimate, 10
Frequent behaviors, daily diaries to assess, 25–26
Future, survey questions about the, 45

G

Generalizability theory (G theory), 122
Going back, on a survey, 42
Grand-mean centering, 117–118
G theory (generalizability theory), 122

I

IDs, participant, 79–80, 99–100
Inattentive responses, 105
Incentives, 136
Infrequent behaviors, daily diaries to assess, 26
Infrequent surveys, 54
In-lab procedures, in research article, 133
In-person visits, 91
Institutional review board (IRB), 65–66
Intensive assessment, importance of, 6, 10–11
Intensive longitudinal methods, 5, 119
Interactive-voice-response (IVR) systems
    about, 56
    contingency plans when using, 75
    conveniency of, 62–63
    preparation for use of, 72
    security of, 66
Interval-contingent sampling, 22
Intraclass correlation (ICC)
    about, 115–116
    and estimating reliability, 121–122
    and power analysis, 124
    in research article, 133, 137
IRB (institutional review board), 65–66
Items, survey
    assembling, 46–48
    complexity of, 42
    developing, 38–46
    estimating reliability of, 121
    factors of, affecting survey duration, 42
    length of, 42
    missing by, 104
    presentation of, 42
    reducing number of, 39, 41
    on self-report surveys, 36–38
Items per screen, 42
IVR systems. *See* Interactive-voice-response systems

J

Journal Article Reporting Standards (JARS), 132
Journals, publishing research in, 131

K

Karwowski, M., 28
Key variables, 101

L

Lab research, 6–7
Lagged time, 96
Laurenceau, J. P., 109, 122
Law, M. K., 22
Linking records, 70
Long format, of data files, 76, 97–98
Longitudinal methods, daily life methods vs., 13

M

Manual, for research team, 81, 83
Many-facet Rasch modeling (MFRM), 123
MAR (missing at random), 103
Matching cases, 101
Maximum likelihood (ML), 137
MCAR (missingness completely at random), 103
McKnight, P. E., 103
Measurement reactivity, 48–51
Mehl, M. R., 4
Merging data files, 99–102
Metaconsciousness, 9–10, 21
Methods section, 132–136
MFRM (many-facet Rasch modeling), 123
Missed surveys, 61–62, 86, 113
Missing at random (MAR), 103
Missing by beep, 104
Missing by item, 104
Missing by person, 103–104
Missing data, 102–103
Missingness completely at random (MCAR), 103
Missing not at random (MNAR), 103
ML (maximum likelihood), 137
MNAR (missing not at random), 103
Modeling, describing methods of, 133, 137
Modern experience sampling, 25
Monitoring survey activity, 87–88, 135–136
Monte Carlo simulations, 124–125
Motivation for change, 50
Multilevel regression analysis, 117

N

Narrow sampling, 18
Natural environments, importance of assessment in, 4, 6–7
NEO Personality Inventory-3 Extraversion subscale, 121
Nested observations, 113–117
Nezlek, J. B., 19–20, 121
Nonindependent observations, 113–117
Nonmatching cases, 101
Nonresponse, factors affecting, 89–92
Non–self-report methods, 66
Number of items, 39

O

Observations, nested and nonindependent, 113–117
Onboarding sessions, 81
Online surveys, 25, 64
Openness to Experience, 7
Open science, 138
Open Science Framework project, 138
Optimal Design, 123
Organizing data, 93–102
    cleaning up data files, 95–96
    merging data files, 99–102
    restructuring data files, 96–99
    taking stock of files, 94
Out-of-lab procedures, 133
Overinclusive sampling, 113

P

Palm Pilot research, as term, 5
Palm Pilots, 56–58, 63
Paper surveys, 56, 91
Papp, L. M., 20
Participant(s)
    addressing experience of, in research presentations, 130
    assigning IDs to, 79–80, 99–100
    burden on, in random-interval sampling, 31
    check-ins with, 88
    common questions of, 73
    control of signal by, 58–59
    convenience for, 62–63
    and data security, 67
    describing, in methods section, 132–133
    describing training of, in methods section, 135

excluding, 106–109
fit for, 64–65
monitoring compliance of, 87
recruitment of, 81
signaling, 54–55
teaching, about study, 70, 84–86
and time stamping, 60
training of, 65
unequal participation with, 112–113
using devices of, for collecting data, 58
Participation, unequal, 112–114
Passive sampling strategies, active vs., 32
Passive time-stamping methods, 60
Past, survey questions about the, 43–44
Person-mean centering, 117–118
Phillips, M. M., 27–28
Phone calls, signaling participants through, 55
Phones, collecting surveys through, 56. *See also* Devices
Piloting your study, 70, 72–74, 76–78
Planning sample size, 123–125
Power analyses, 123–125
Preferred Reporting Items for Systematic Reviews and Meta-Analyses (PRISMA) guidelines, 132
Preparation for study, 70–83
  evaluating pilot's data files, 76–78
  linking records, 78–80
  making contingency plans, 74–75
  nailing down signals and surveys, 70–72
  piloting data collection, 72–74
  training research staff, 80–83
Present, survey questions about the, 44–45
Presenting research, 128–131
Prestudy awareness, 50
PRISMA (Preferred Reporting Items for Systematic Reviews and Meta-Analyses) guidelines, 132
Privacy, data, 65–67
PsyArXiv, 138
Psychology, consumer, 77
Public archives, 138
Publishing research, 131–138
  methods section, 132–136
  results section, 136–138

Q

Quality, data. *See* Data quality

R

Random-interval sampling, 27–32
Randomization, 42, 47–48
Random responses, 105–106
Random signaling, 30
Rasch models, 123
Reactivity, measurement, 48–51
Real-time data capture. *See also* Daily life methods
  importance of, 6, 8–10
  as term, 5
Recall biases, 9, 26–27
Regression analysis, 112–113, 117
Reis, H. T., 6, 22
Reliability, estimating, 121–123
Remote data collection, 84
Removing constructs, 39
Repeated assessments, 48–49
Repetition, of daily life surveys, 35
Research, presenting and publishing, 128–138
Research assistants, 83, 86
Research questions, for daily life methods, 14–15
Research staff, training, 70, 80–83
Response rates
  checking in to increase, 88–89
  describing, in research article, 133
  description of, in results section, 136–137
  and excluding participants, 106–107
  improving, 89–91
  study design factors influencing, 91
  survey factors influencing, 89–90
Responses
  capturing, 42, 95
  confirming, 42
  inattentive, 105
  random, 105–106
  rate of. *See* Response rates
Restructuring data files, 96–99
Results section, 133, 136–138
Retrospective self-reports, 8–9
Rings, signaling participants through, 55
Running the study, 83–89
  checking in during the study, 88–89
  monitoring survey activity, 87–88
  teaching participants about study, 84–86

S

Salience, 21, 90
Sample size, 123–125

Sample surveys, for presentations, 128
Sampling, 17–33
   active vs. passive, 32
   broad, 18
   combining types of, 31–33
   continuous, 32
   from daily life, 17–19
   describing, in methods section, 132–134
   event-based. *See* Event-based sampling
   experience, 28, 46. *See also* Random-interval sampling
   fixed-interval. *See* Fixed-interval sampling
   narrow, 18
   overinclusive, 113
   random-interval, 27–32
   signal-contingent, 28. *See also* Random-interval sampling
   time-based, 19, 113
   within-day. *See* Within-day sampling
Sampling frame, 113
Screening out data, 104–109
Script, for research teams, 81–82
Seasonal clock changes, 61
Security, data, 65–67
Segal's Law, 61
Self-report surveys, 35–51
   about, 35–36
   days, beeps, and items on, 36–38
   developing items for, 38–46
   features of, 46–48
   and measurement reactivity, 48–51
   "near-time" data collection with, 8
   outcomes beyond, 8
   privacy of, 66
   retrospective, 8–9
Serial order, 95, 119
Short scales, 39–40
Signal-contingent sampling, 28. *See also* Random-interval sampling
Signals
   common methods for, 54–55
   common participant questions about, 73
   describing, in methods section, 134–135
   participant control of, 58–59, 90
   preparation for, 70–71
   random, 30
   serial order of, 95
   as time anchors, 44
   time stamps for, 59
Smartphones, 55–57
Smart Richman, L., 28

SMS text messages
   collecting surveys through, 56
   signaling participants through, 55
Social interactions, event-based sampling for, 20
Society for Ambulatory Assessment, 5
Speeding up a survey, 41
Statistics, descriptive, 102, 133, 137
Subsetting, 42
Survey methods, daily life methods vs., 12–13
Surveys
   common participant questions about, 73
   common ways of collecting, 56
   conveniency of, 62–63
   deciding how to send out, 70–71
   describing design of, in methods section, 132–134
   dropping single, from data set, 105
   duration of, 41–42, 105
   items on. *See* Items
   length of, 38–39, 47, 90
   measuring intuitiveness/convenience through time of, 62
   missed, 61–62, 86, 113
   monitoring, 87–88
   online, 25, 64
   paper, 56, 91
   for random-interval sampling, 29–30
   sample, for presentations, 128
   self-report. *See* Self-report surveys
   signaling participants for infrequent, 54
   signals for. *See* Signals
   time stamping, 59–60
   trait, 43
System
   defined, 53
   describing, in methods section, 134–135
   and response rate, 91
   selecting a. *See* System selection considerations
System selection considerations, 53–67
   convenience for participants, 62–63
   data privacy and security, 65–67
   equipment, 55–58
   fit for participants and environment, 64–65
   initial and ongoing costs, 63–64
   missed surveys, 61–62
   participant control of signal, 58–59
   personnel and participant training, 65
   sending signals or collecting data, 54–55
   time stamping, 59–61

T

Taking stock of files, 94
TAM, 123
Technical issues, 73
Technology
    monitoring, 87–88
    pilot testing, 76
    preparation for use of, 71–72
    training research team for use of, 82
Testing team, 73–74
Text messages. *See* SMS text messages
Theft, 57
Time
    coding, 119
    daily life methods used to assess, 14
    deciding how to represent, 95–96
    defining, in survey questions, 43–45
    intervals of, 96
    in longitudinal studies, 13
    response rates affected by, 91
    understanding and defining, 119–120
Time anchors, 43–44
Time-based sampling, 19, 113
Time referencing, 36, 43
Time stamping, 59–61, 105
Time-to-event, 96
"Time zero" event, 96
Time zones, 60

Traditional self-report scales, 38–39, 41
Training, 65
    for research staff, 70, 80–83
Trait surveys, 43

U

Undergraduate students, presentations by, 131
Unequal participation, 112–114
Usability testing, 74

V

Variability, assessing, 14–15

W

Web surveys, 56, 64, 75
Wheeler, L., 19–20
Wide format, of data files, 76, 97–98
Within-day fixed intervals, 23–24, 120
Within-day sampling
    end-of-day survey combined with, 100
    participant device use for, 58
    signaling participants for, 54
Within-person level
    of daily diaries, 114
    daily life methods used to assess, 15
Wray, T. B., 90

About the Authors

Paul J. Silvia, PhD, is the Lucy Spinks Keker Excellence Professor at the University of North Carolina at Greensboro, where he has been conducting experience sampling and daily diary research since the days when Palm Pilots were high tech. He has studied daily life experiences in many clinical and community groups, including older adults, veterans, parents adjudicated for child maltreatment, and adults with depression, attention-deficit/hyperactivity disorder, or posttraumatic stress disorder. In addition to self-report projects, he has conducted experience sampling studies that integrate neuroimaging and ambulatory cardiac monitoring.

Katherine N. Cotter, PhD, is a postdoctoral fellow with the Humanities and Human Flourishing Project at the Positive Psychology Center at the University of Pennsylvania. Her work emphasizes the study of aesthetics and the arts in people's everyday environments, using both experience sampling and daily diary techniques. Her recent work involves field research within art museums to understand people's aesthetic experiences within the museum context.